FEB 0 2 2018

Muskegon Area District Library

fun and important
stories to know!

D1400640

ISBN-13: 978-1-945470-26-4

Published by WorthyKids/Ideals, an imprint of Worthy Publishing Group, a division of Worthy Media, Inc., in association with Museum of the Bible.

museum of the Bible

BOOKS

Copyright © 2017 by Museum of the Bible Books
409 3rd St. SW
Washington, D.C. 20024-4706
Museum of the Bible is an innovative, global, educational institution whose purpose is to invite all people to engage with the history, narrative, and impact of the Bible.

All rights reserved. No part of this publication may be reproduced or transmitted in any form or by any means, electronic or mechanical, including photocopy, recording, or any information storage and retrieval system, without permission in writing from the publisher.

WorthyKids/Ideals is a registered trademark of Worthy Media, Inc.

Library of Congress CIP data is on file

Unless otherwise indicated, scripture quotations are from the ESV® Bible (The Holy Bible, English Standard Version®), copyright © 2001 by Crossway, a publishing ministry of Good News Publishers. Used by permission. All rights reserved.

Scripture quotations marked (NIV) are taken from the Holy Bible, New International Version®, NIV®. Copyright © 1973, 1978, 1984, 2011 by Biblica, Inc.™ Used by permission of Zondervan. All rights reserved worldwide. www.zondervan.com. The "NIV" and "New International Version" are trademarks registered in the United States Patent and Trademark Office by Biblica, Inc.™

Scripture quotations marked NLT are taken from the Holy Bible, New Living Translation, copyright © 1996, 2004, 2007, 2013 by Tyndale House Foundation. Used by permission of Tyndale House Publishers, Inc., Carol Stream, Illinois, 60188. All rights reserved.

Produced with the assistance of Hudson Bible (www.HudsonBible.com)
Front cover images: water, © Lorelyn Medina/Adobe Stock; camel, © Martin M303/Adobe Stock; donkey, © Alvaro/Adobe Stock; grasshopper, © guy/Adobe Stock.
Back cover images: lizard, © PetlinDmitry/Shutterstock; frog, © Smit/Shutterstock; bee, © Peter Waters/Shutterstock; waves, © RockSweeper/Shutterstock.

Printed and bound in the U.S.A.
RRD-Craw_Sep17_1

Wild and Wacky Things in the Bible

fun and important stories to know!

written by
April LoTempio

Worthy kids
ideals®

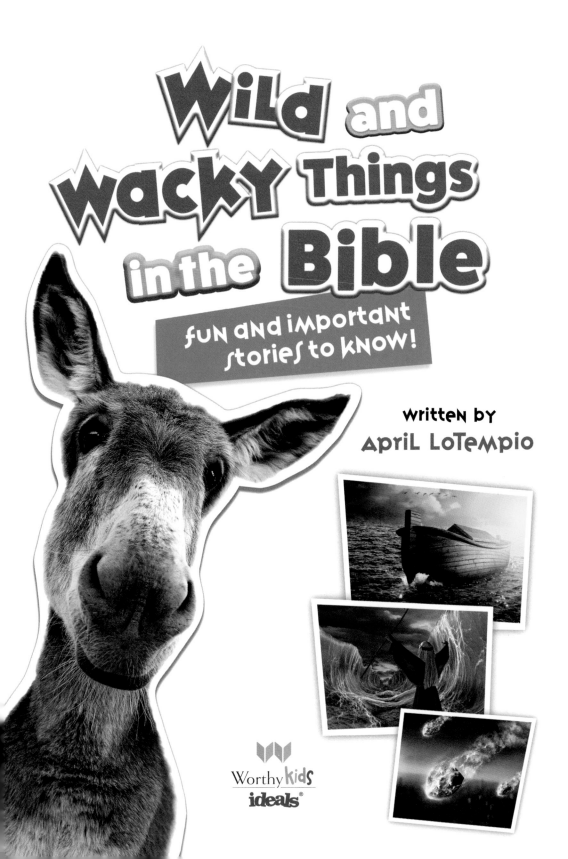

Contents

1 CREATION

2 NOT-SO-ORDINARY ANIMALS

3 OUTRAGEOUS FOOD

4 ICKY DISEASES

5 SURPRISING VICTORIES

6 THESE PEOPLE DID WHAT?

7 OUT-OF-THIS-WORLD APPEARANCES

8 THE DEAD BECOME ALIVE AGAIN

9 WACKY WATER TALES

10 DREAMS AND VISIONS

11 UNUSUAL HUMANS

12 UNNATURAL ACTS OF NATURE

13 EXTRAORDINARY EVENTS

Introduction

The Bible isn't just the best-selling book of all time. It is the best-selling book of the year—every year. It's also the most translated and distributed book in the world. What makes this ancient text so popular?

Stranger-than-fiction events fill the pages of the Bible, beginning on the first page with the story of creation. Hundreds of chapters follow that contain stories of wild and wacky happenings: Animals talk. People are miraculously healed. Unexplainable weather occurs. God raises the dead, punishes the wicked, and speaks through dreams and visions.

Dive into tales of superhuman strength, overwhelming plagues, heavenly beings, and epic battles. You might recognize some well-known stories like David and Goliath or Noah's ark. Perhaps you'll be surprised by lesser-known tales, such as King Belshazzar and the floating hand or the prophet Elisha's poisonous stew. Compare these events with modern science and culture through sidebars like "Fast Facts" and "Did You Know?"

Enjoy this wild and wacky spin on some of the Bible's most amazing events.

God Creates!

Genesis 1:1–2:3

Have you ever created something with your own hands? Maybe you used paints and paper to create a picture. Or maybe you mixed ingredients like flour and eggs to make a cake. Or maybe you used pieces of wood to build a treehouse. Well, God created the heavens and the earth!

How did God do it? Genesis 1 shows that God spoke words. When the world was completely dark, God said, "Let there be light." And light appeared! He spoke of sky and earth, seas and plants, fish and birds and animals. And they appeared! In six days, God created the entire universe and everything in it.

"Then God said, 'Let there be a space between the waters, to separate the waters of the heavens from the waters of the earth.' And that is what happened." Genesis 1:6–7 (NLT)

did you KNOW?

Every physical thing is made of matter. Matter is anything that takes up space and has mass (or weight). Bricks and feathers and water are all matter. Ideas and feelings are not matter. Even one tiny atom is matter. Atoms are so small that millions of them fit on the tip of a sharpened pencil! Scientists agree that matter cannot be created or destroyed; it can only be changed. That idea is a law in science. The first book of many versions of the Bible says, "In the beginning, God created the heavens and the earth." Some people believe this means God created matter out of nothing. Many people believe God even created the science that shows us what matter is all about.

Even one tiny atom is matter.

Genesis 1 tells us that God created everything over a period of six days. Here's the order of God's creation:

1st Day	Light
2nd Day	Sky
3rd Day	Land (earth) and seas (water), plants
4th Day	Sun, moon, stars
5th Day	Fish and birds (animals of the sea and sky)
6th Day	Land animals and humans

A Day of Rest

People sometimes talk about "creation week" or "six days of creation." How long did it take for God to create everything? The Bible says that God spent six days creating everything. Then, on the seventh day he rested. "God blessed the seventh day and made it holy" (Genesis 2:3). Some other biblical writers used this as a reason for having a day of rest. The Bible calls this day the Sabbath, a day set aside for the people to rest and to worship God. Today, many Jews and Christians set apart one day of Sabbath rest each week to refrain from work and to attend churches and synagogues.

The Man Who Was Never Born

Genesis 2:5–20

Think of the men you know—uncles, teachers, neighbors, coaches. Every single one was once born as a tiny baby. It took years for them to grow into men. But the first man, Adam, seems to have skipped that step.

In the book of Genesis, when God created Adam on the sixth day of creation, he did something different. God created all the rest of creation—including the sun, plants, and animals—out of nothing. And each appeared when God spoke. But God made Adam out of dust from the ground. Then he breathed life into Adam's nose. Adam was alive!

God placed him in the garden of Eden, where he had plenty of food to eat and important work to do.

God made Adam out of dust from the ground.

did you KNOW?

Adam lived in a beautiful garden. But he probably didn't just sit around smelling flowers all day. He probably didn't spend all this time taking naps under the trees. God gave him jobs to do. First, Adam worked as a gardener. He took care of the plants and trees in the garden of Eden. Adam also had the special task of giving names to all the animals. Genesis 2:19 tells us that God brought "every beast of the field and every bird of the heavens" to Adam, who gave them names. He must have had fun naming all the animals!

FAST FACTS

The average grown man in the United States

- is **5** feet **9 1/2** inches tall
- weighs **195** pounds
- has about **100,000** heartbeats per day
- takes about **23,000** breaths per day

Adam had the special task of giving names to all the animals.

God Creates the First Woman

Genesis 2:18–25

After God created the first man, Adam, he felt that something—or someone—was still missing. Adam had seen and named every animal, but not one was a suitable partner for him. So God went to work on another creation.

This time, God didn't speak or use dust. Instead, God put Adam into a deep sleep. He opened up Adam's side, took out one of his ribs, closed up the skin, and created a woman from the rib. When Adam woke up, he saw a woman for the first time!

When Adam woke up, he saw a woman for the first time!

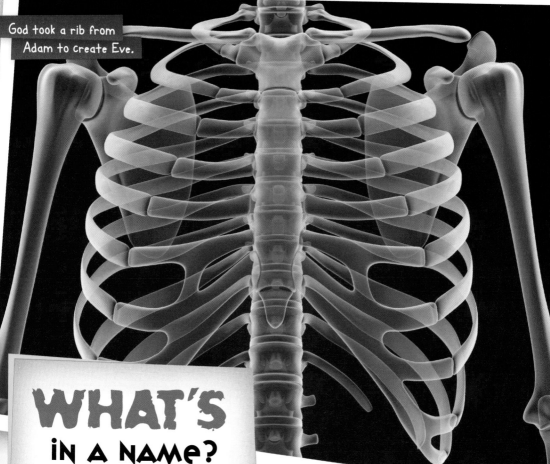

God took a rib from Adam to create Eve.

WHAT'S iN A NAMe?

Adam chose the name *Eve* for his wife. This name means "life."

Some of the most popular baby names in recent years come from the Bible—Noah, James, Elijah, and Abigail. However, the names *Adam* and *Eve* are not as popular today in the United States. (In 2017 Adam was the 30th most popular name for baby boys, and Eve was the 412th most popular name for baby girls).

One Less Rib in Boys?

Some people think baby boys are born with one less rib than baby girls, since God took a rib from Adam to create Eve. But that's not true. Boys and girls have the same number of ribs.

Frogs in the Bed and Flies in the Soup

Exodus 7–11

Some would say there's nothing better than a fluffy puppy—except maybe *two* fluffy puppies! What about an entire roomful of puppies? A whole house filled with animals might be fun, unless of course the animals are frogs or flies or other insects. But that's exactly what God gave the Egyptians in the book of Exodus.

Pharaoh eventually let the Israelites go—but not before the Egyptians had to put up with many creepy-crawly animals.

Exodus describes a time when the Egyptians held the Israelites captive as slaves. The Egyptian king, Pharaoh, refused to set them free. God sent Moses to talk to Pharaoh. Moses asked Pharaoh many times to let God's people go. But Pharaoh refused again and again. Each time, God sent plagues to the Egyptians to show his power. Once he turned all the water in the Nile River to blood. Another time he sent hail that destroyed crops. Several times he sent living creatures as plagues on the Egyptians.

God sent frogs that filled the Egyptians' homes. They crawled up out of the Nile River. The frogs likely got into people's beds and mixing bowls. They probably hopped on the people. When God let the frogs die, the Egyptians had to gather them into big, smelly piles.

After the frogs, God sent gnats. All the dust on the ground became flying, biting gnats. They covered the Egyptians and their animals. Still, Pharaoh would not listen to God.

Then God sent flies. Flies covered the ground, the homes, and the people of Egypt. But God protected the Israelites and kept the flies away from them. Still, Pharaoh's heart was hard and he would not let the Israelites go.

Later God sent locusts. The east wind brought so many locusts that the land was dark. Locusts covered the entire ground. They ate every plant and the fruit on all the trees in Egypt. Still, Pharaoh would not let the Israelites go free.

Pharaoh eventually let the Israelites go — but not before the Egyptians had to put up with many creepy-crawly animals. Think of that the next time a fly buzzes into your house!

did you KNOW?

In the summer of 1874, a massive swarm of locusts attacked the Great Plains of the United States. They filled the sky and then landed on farm crops. People tied strings around their pant legs to keep the locusts from crawling up their legs! Farmers tried to cover their crops with sheets and blankets, but the locusts ate those too. The locusts ate wool right off the sheep! They also ate through leather, paint, and wood. The locusts left farmers with nothing to eat, no crops to sell, and no food for their animals.

FAST FACTS

A group of frogs is called an **army**.

A housefly **poops** almost every time it lands.

A gnat can lay up to **300 eggs** in one day.

A swarm of locusts can be up to **460 square miles** in size — that's almost as big as the city of **Los Angeles**, California, USA!

Blame It on the Goat

Leviticus 16:7–22

Leviticus describes the Israelites living in the wilderness. As they traveled, they would set up a tent (called the tabernacle) as their meeting place to worship God. Priests performed ceremonies in the tabernacle. One of their ceremonies each year involved a special goat, called the scapegoat.

On the Day of Atonement, the Israelites remembered their sins. The Bible names different types of sins. Some are about acting, or not acting, in certain ways. Some are about doing, or not doing, certain things God has commanded.

The scapegoat was a symbol representing the removal of sin.

During Yom Kippur people often wear white as a symbol of being cleansed from sin.

On that Day of Atonement the people brought two goats to the tabernacle, where the priest would "cast lots" (like flipping a coin). One goat was sacrificed and offered to God. The other goat became the scapegoat.

The priest placed his hands on the scapegoat's head. He spoke out loud all the sins of the people, as a symbolic way of putting the sins on the goat's head. Then the goat was taken far away and released into the wilderness.

The scapegoat was a symbol to the Israelites. It represented the removal of their sin.

Yom Kippur

Perhaps you've heard of the Jewish holiday called Yom Kippur. It's the modern-day observance of the Day of Atonement. On this special day, people do not work or eat. The community spends time in prayer and confession, admitting the things they have done to disobey God. Prayers are spoken using "we" instead of "I." Often, people wear white as a symbol of being cleansed from sin.

A Talking Donkey

Numbers 22:21–33

Just imagine how cool it would be to hear an animal talk. Your cat could tell you which treats he or she likes best. A squirrel could ask if it's safe to cross the street. A donkey could tell you when you're not treating her with kindness— like in the story of Balaam.

Balaam was a prophet of God, but he didn't always do what was right. Carrying Balaam to the land of Moab, Balaam's donkey suddenly veered off the road into a field. Balaam angrily beat his donkey, forcing it back onto the road. Soon after, the donkey pressed up against a wall, crushing Balaam's foot. For a second time, Balaam beat his donkey. Then, the donkey lay down in the road, refusing to go on. Balaam beat the donkey a third time.

Just imagine how cool it would be to hear an animal talk. This happened to Balaam

LEARNING LANGUAGES

Speaking and writing aren't the only types of communication people use. Search online or in a library book for these different alphabets. Can you learn to spell your name in each?

- Sign Language
- Braille
- Nautical flags
- Morse code

What was going on? Numbers 22 says that God sent a sword-carrying angel to stand in the road, blocking Balaam's way. The donkey could see the angel, but Balaam could not.

Finally, after three beatings, the donkey miraculously opened her mouth and spoke to Balaam, asking why he was beating her. "What have I done to you?" she asked.

Balaam was so angry that he didn't think about the startling fact that his donkey could talk. Instead, he wished for a sword in his hand so he could kill her.

The donkey asked, "Is it my habit to treat you this way?"

"No," Balaam admitted. Then God opened Balaam's eyes, and he could see the angel in the road. Balaam learned

Can Animals Talk?

Animals certainly communicate with one another. They use barks, chirps, squeaks, and roars to send warnings or find a mate. Some primates have learned to use sign language to communicate with humans. But what about human speech? A few animals, especially parrots, can mimic human speech. However, copying human sounds and understanding speech are two different things.

that the angel would have killed him but the donkey had saved his life. What do you think Balaam should have said then to his talking donkey?

Ravens That Deliver Dinner

1 Kings 17:1–6

Stretch your arms as wide as you can. From fingertip to fingertip, that's about the wingspan of a raven. Ravens are large black birds with wingspans that measure up to four feet. They are very intelligent. According to laws given by God to the Israelites, ravens were considered unclean and not to be eaten.

Imagine, then, the surprise of Elijah (an Israelite prophet) when God said the ravens would feed him! Commanded by God to hide in the

Imagine the surprise of Elijah when he learned that ravens would deliver his meals!

14

top
of the class

Scientists don't agree on exactly which animals are the smartest, but here are some animals that usually make the top ten:

- Primates (like chimpanzees, orangutans, gorillas, and monkeys)
- Killer whales
- Dolphins
- Elephants
- Pigs
- Ravens, crows, and pigeons
- Octopi
- Rats
- Squirrels
- Raccoons

wilderness, Elijah depended on these birds to survive. Elijah did not eat the ravens. Instead, they brought him bread and meat each morning and each evening.

This is not normal bird behavior. Ravens are scavengers, meaning they eat anything, including dead animals. They do not typically find bread and meat and deliver it to hiding prophets. But 1 Kings 17 tells us that Elijah and the ravens did what God told them to do.

A Raven Named Grip

Charles Dickens is a British author famous for writing *A Christmas Carol*. During his lifetime, he kept a pet raven named Grip. Like other ravens, Grip could imitate human speech. It learned several words. It even inspired a character—a raven named Grip—in one of Dickens's books. At one point, Dickens (along with Grip) met the American author Edgar Allan Poe. Shortly after their meeting, Poe wrote his most famous poem, "The Raven."

The Bullies and the Bears

2 Kings 2:23–25

Have you ever heard the saying "Sticks and stones may break my bones, but words will never hurt me"? It's a silly thing people say, because name-calling usually does hurt people. One of the strangest stories in the Bible involves some name-calling and two vicious bears.

Elisha, God's prophet in Israel, was on his way to the city of Bethel. More than forty boys appeared and began mocking Elisha. They called him "baldhead." This this was disrespectful and insulting.

Elisha cursed them in the name of the Lord. God sent an unusual punishment: Two female bears

The boys called Elisha "baldhead." This was disrespectful and insulting.

appeared out of the woods. They attacked the boys, mauling forty-two of them. Likely the people of Bethel took notice of this new prophet and his powerful God.

Bears Around the World

There are eight species of bear, including the polar bear, black bear, brown bear, and giant panda. Bears live in the Americas, Europe, and Asia, but almost always in the northern hemisphere. The bears from the book of 2 Kings were most likely Syrian brown bears, which no longer live in Israel. They may have weighed 550 pounds each. Though they aren't the largest bears, Syrian brown bears can be very fierce.

dANgerous BEASTS

If trained from a young age, bears can become tame and even perform circus tricks. But don't be fooled; bears in the wild are dangerous. Some bears stand over eight feet tall and run thirty-five miles per hour. They are most likely to attack when startled, if near a food source, or when they are with their cubs. However, bear attacks are rare, especially now that their populations have grown smaller. Bears almost never attack a large group of people, as they did in the biblical story.

A Most Unusual Fish

Jonah 1–3

Trying to hide what you've done wrong seldom works. Jonah discovered this the hard way.

The people of Nineveh were up to no good. Someone needed to talk to them about their evil actions, and that someone was Jonah. But when God commanded Jonah to go to Nineveh, Jonah hopped on a ship heading the opposite way.

The Bible says that God sent a terrible storm to toss the ship. The frightened sailors cried out to their gods. Jonah admitted it was his fault. "Hurl me into the sea," he urged them. The sailors hesitated. Finally, they tossed Jonah overboard. The storm calmed, and a large fish swallowed Jonah. He prayed and cried out for God to help him. For three days and three nights, Jonah lived inside the fish. After the three days and three nights, the fish spit Jonah up onto land. Jonah was ready to obey God.

This time, Jonah did what God had instructed him to do. The Bible tells us

We don't know exactly what kind of fish swallowed Jonah.

Jonah went to Nineveh and warned the people that their city would be destroyed because they had disobeyed God. The people listened to Jonah and were sorry for their wicked ways.

We don't know exactly what kind of fish swallowed Jonah. A whale shark? A blue whale? A special fish that God created just for this task? In fact, there's much we can't figure out about this event. How did Jonah breathe? Why wasn't he crushed or hurt by the fish's stomach acid?

The Bible doesn't give us those answers, but it does tell us the end of the story—the people of Nineveh believed God and repented. God responded with mercy and spared the city.

did you KNOW?

The largest living land animal is the elephant. The largest living sea animal is the blue whale. A blue whale is about the size of three school buses! But the Bible mentions some beasts that might have been even bigger. *Leviathan* was some kind of sea serpent, and *behemoth* was a land animal. Were these just different names for well-known animals, like a crocodile or an apatosaurus? Or are these animals that scientists have yet to discover? What do you think?

A Hungry Worm

After preaching in Nineveh, Jonah was upset because God did not destroy Nineveh. Jonah sat under the shade of a plant God provided to protect him from the heat of the sun. But the next day, God sent a worm to damage the plant. With the sun beating down on him, Jonah was even more upset. God used the worm to teach Jonah. Just as Jonah did not want the plant to be destroyed, God did not want the people in Nineveh to be destroyed.

Jonah sat under the shade of a plant God provided to protect him from the heat.

The Same Breakfast for Forty Years

Exodus 16

Soon after the Israelites left Egypt, they started grumbling. In a place called the wilderness of Sin, they complained to Moses that they would starve to death.

But, the Israelites did not starve. God provided food for them. In the evening, quail came and covered their camp. These birds would be a good source of meat. In the morning, God provided manna.

What is manna? That's what the Israelites wanted to know! In fact, the word *manna* might mean "What is it?" They had never before seen this strange bread from heaven. It appeared on the ground in the early morning, once the dew was gone. After a short time, it melted away in the hot sun.

Quail provided a good source of meat for the Israelites.

did You KNOW?

Scientists and historians have different ideas about what manna could have been. Some say it's a kind of sap from the tamarisk shrub that grows in the desert. Others think it's really a secretion from bugs that live on this plant. Still others think manna was a kind of dried algae that the wind carried to the desert.

The Bible tells us manna was white. It might have been thin flakes or small and round like seeds. It tasted like wafers made with honey. The Israelites could bake and boil it. However, they could not save it overnight. When they tried to save the manna, it became smelly and filled with maggots. Yuck!

Some say manna is part of the story to show that God takes care of people who follow him only. God told Moses the manna would come. The manna stopped appearing once the Israelites left the wilderness. Perhaps most surprising of all, manna did not appear on the Sabbath. On the seventh day of the week, when the Israelites were to rest from their work, there was no manna. Instead, they collected extra manna on the sixth day—that was the only day they could keep manna overnight without it rotting.

Day after day, the Israelites ate manna for breakfast. Sometimes they complained about having the same old thing every morning (Numbers 11:6). But because of manna, the Israelites survived living in the wilderness for forty years.

What's For Breakfast?

People eat breakfast at home, at school, and even in the car. These are the three most popular breakfast foods in the United States:

1. Cold cereal
2. Eggs
3. Breads

What's your favorite food to eat for breakfast?

A Strange Container for Honey

Judges 14:5–18

What's a seven-letter word that contains hundreds of letters? *Mailbox*! Don't you just love riddles? So did Samson. In the book of Judges in the Bible we read this riddle he told a bunch of people at his wedding:

*Out of the eater
came something to eat.
Out of the strong
came something sweet.*

Samson told thirty wedding guests that if they could solve his riddle, he would give them thirty shirts and thirty changes of clothes to wear. But if they could not solve the riddle, they would have to give him thirty shirts and thirty changes of clothes.

Some time before his wedding, Samson was attacked by a lion.

Honey is tasty but what if it came fr the body of a dead li

However, the lion was no match for Samson's strength. Samson killed the lion by tearing it open with his bare hands.

Later on, as Samson was on his way to get married, he saw the lion's body and found something unusual: it was swarming with bees! Inside the body, the bees had made honey. Samson scooped out the honey with his hands and ate it. He also gave some to his parents. But he never told them about killing the lion or that the honey had come from the dead lion's body.

Eating something out of a rotting animal might sound pretty gross to you, and it is! But Samson shouldn't have eaten the honey for another reason. The Israelites were commanded by God to follow a law that forbade them from touching a carcass. But Samson didn't just touch the dead lion; he reached inside its body to scoop the honey!

Nazirites in the Bible

Samson was a Nazirite, which means he was dedicated to God from his birth and had to follow some special rules, like never cutting his hair or drinking wine. The prophet Samuel (1 Samuel 1:11) and John the Baptist (Luke 1:13–15) were also considered Nazirites.

FAST FACTS

Honeybees buzz because their wings beat about **230 times per minute**.

A worker bee lives only **five to six weeks**, while the queen bee can live up to **five years**.

A queen bee can lay over **two thousand eggs** per day.

Samson not only broke his commitment to God but also lost the bet. The wedding guests convinced Samson's wife to help them cheat to solve the riddle, saying:

What is sweeter than honey?
What is stronger than a lion?

Samson had many reasons to be troubled. He'd deceived his parents, broken God's rule, been betrayed by his wife, and lost the bet—all for a scoop of honey.

Poisonous Gourd Stew

2 Kings 4:38–41

Do you like to try new foods? If you've never seen the food before, you probably want to know what it is before you taste it.

A story in the book of 2 Kings tells us there was a famine in the land of Israel, and many people didn't have enough to eat. However, the prophet Elisha told his servant to make stew for him and the men traveling with them. The servant went out to the fields to pick herbs, and there he found a vine bursting with wild gourds. Even though he didn't know what they were, he hurried home with the gourds to make stew.

The men began to eat the stew. Suddenly, the men cried out to Elisha, "There is death in the pot!" They could not eat the stew.

Quickly, Elisha called for some flour and threw it into the pot. He told the servant to serve the stew again. This time, the stew was fine and everyone could eat it.

How likely are you to try gourd stew?

did You KNOW?

Many ordinary foods you eat all the time actually contain some poison. However, these toxins are usually found in very small amounts. Nutmeg, almonds, potatoes, apple seeds, and raw honey all have bits of elements considered to be poisonous. The deadliest food, however, is probably the puffer fish. If it is not prepared properly, this fish causes paralysis and death when eaten!

Elisha's Miracles

In 2 Kings, Elisha performed many miracles in addition to fixing poisonous stew. Here are a few of them:

- He parted the waters of the Jordan River by striking it with a cloak (2 Kings 2:14).
- He helped a poor widow fill empty containers with oil to sell (2 Kings 4:1–7).
- He brought a dead boy back to life (2 Kings 4:32–35).
- He healed a man who had leprosy (2 Kings 5:13–14).

Feasting on God's Words

Ezekiel 3:1–4

People say you are what you eat. If that's true, then we might wonder about the prophet Ezekiel, who ate a scroll. Ezekiel 3 tells us about a vision the prophet Ezekiel had. In his vision God told him, "Eat this scroll." Ezekiel obeyed, noting that the scroll tasted "as sweet as honey." But why?

This vision from God prepared Ezekiel to speak to the people of Israel. Before Ezekiel could share God's message with the people, he had to consume it himself first. Maybe the scroll was a symbol of the words God wanted him to say to the people. Maybe it was an actual scroll. Either way, Ezekiel filled up on God's message before speaking it to the Israelites.

Ezekiel filled up on God's message.

Taste and See

As a way to express his confidence in God, King David wrote, "Taste and see that the LORD is good!" (Psalm 34:8). In a prayer to God, a psalmist wrote, "How sweet are your words to my taste, sweeter than honey to my mouth!" (Psalm 119:103).

did you KNOW?

Ezekiel wasn't the only person from the Bible to eat God's words. Both the prophet Jeremiah and the apostle John did the same.

Jeremiah 15:16—"Your words were found, and I ate them, and your words became to me a joy and the delight of my heart, for I am called by your name, O LORD, God of hosts."

Revelation 10:10—"And I took the little scroll from the hand of the angel and ate it. It was sweet as honey in my mouth, but when I had eaten it my stomach was made bitter."

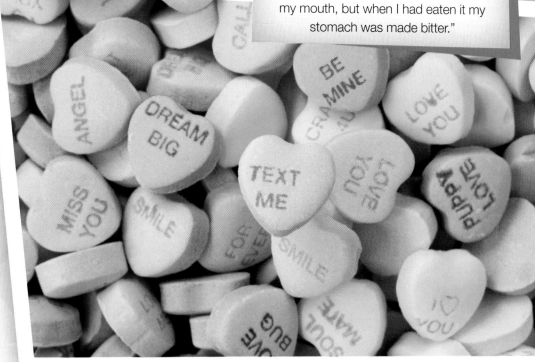

No Bread for Me, Thanks

Ezekiel 4:9–15

Flour, salt, yeast, and water. These are the primary ingredients needed to make bread. Oh, and an oven in which to cook it. While bread recipes can differ, baking in an oven is usually a part of the process—unless you're the prophet Ezekiel.

After commanding Ezekiel in a vision to eat a scroll, God had another unusual command regarding food. The city of Jerusalem was in trouble. The Chaldean army would soon surround the city, cutting off supplies and making food scarce. To prepare the people, God gave Ezekiel some specific commands.

First, Ezekiel would lie on his left side for 390 days. Then he would lie on his right side for 40 days. During this time, he could only eat one special type of bread. The bread was made of wheat, barley, beans, lentils, millet, and emmer, a type of wheat. But the most unusual thing about the bread was the way it would be cooked. Because there would be no other fuel available during the war, God ordered Ezekiel to use human dung (poop) as fuel to cook the bread. Eww!

Ezekiel ate barley cakes baked over cow dung for 430 straight days.

28

Ezekiel Bread

Today, bakeries continue to make bread using the six ingredients included in making Ezekiel's bread. Companies boast that this type of bread is a good source of nutrients and fiber that's easy on digestion. However, baking their bread doesn't involve burning dung!

BIBLICAL Shopping List

Here are some of the most common foods mentioned in the Bible. How many were on your family's shopping list this week?

- Almonds
- Figs
- Grapes
- Salt
- Olives
- Raisins
- Bread, flour, wheat
- Fish
- Calf, goat, lamb, sheep
- Butter
- Cheese
- Milk
- Eggs
- Honey

Humans have used dried animal dung as fuel for fire for thousands of years. But using human dung was one command that Ezekiel just couldn't stomach. He had always followed God's commands for cleanliness. He talked to God about it. So God allowed Ezekiel to use cow dung to bake the bread.

And so Ezekiel did. He ate barley cakes baked over cow dung for 430 straight days. That should give you new appreciation for the oven in your home!

Covered with Sores

Job 2:4–13, 7:5, 42:10–17

It didn't seem like things could get any worse for Job. He'd already lost his thousands of cattle, his servants, and all ten of his children. And things were about to get worse.

The Bible tells us in Job 2:3 that Job was a "blameless and upright man" who turned "away from evil." To test his good character, God let Job become the target of Satan's attacks. Satan struck Job's flocks and family, hoping this would turn Job against God. But that didn't happen. Job refused to curse God, despite all the terrible things that happened to him. So Satan went one step further.

Satan gave Job painful sores, like blisters. They spread from the tips of his toes to the top of his head, covering his whole body. The sores must have been itchy, too, because Job scratched at them with a piece of broken pottery. He couldn't sleep at night. He couldn't work during the day. When Job's friends approached from a distance, they hardly recognized their friend under all those scabs.

Believe it or not, things got even worse for Job. The sores became infected, oozing and cracking Job's skin. Job's condition was so bad, he preferred death to life.

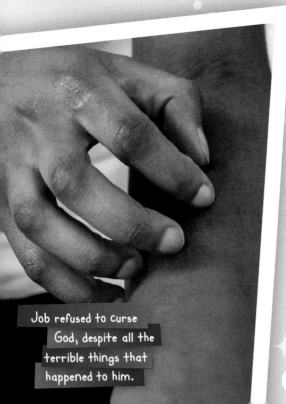

Job refused to curse God, despite all the terrible things that happened to him.

Job did recover. At the end of the book of Job, we find out that God also gave Job twice as many cattle as he had before and another ten children. Job lived well into old age and hopefully never had so much as a blister again!

did You KNOW?

The book of Job might be the oldest one in the Bible (though it is not placed first).

The name *Job* can mean "the persecuted one."

Job lived to be about two hundred years old.

Medically Speaking

In Job 7:5, Job says, "My flesh is clothed with worms and dirt." Human skin can become infested with maggots, or fly larvae. Known as *myiasis*, this skin infection happens when fly eggs come in contact with skin and the newly hatched larvae burrow inside. This can form itchy boils, like those described in the book of Job. Eventually, the larvae grow and exit the skin through an open wound. But don't worry, *myiasis* is rare—a bump on your skin doesn't mean there are larvae inside!

Bad Advice

When Job's wife saw her husband covered in sores and suffering, she told him to "curse God and die" (Job 2:9). Three friends who came to visit all suspected Job was being punished for sin. They told Job to admit he did something wrong. So Job not only suffered at the hands of Satan but also put up with bad advice from those closest to him!

Caring for the Skin You're In

Leviticus 13

Priests had an important job in ancient Israel. They were in charge of offerings, ceremonies, and checking people's skin diseases. You read that right—priests had to check skin diseases! In fact, an entire book of the Bible (Leviticus) teaches about staying clean in God's sight. Parts of that book deal with skin diseases.

Remember, the Israelites wandered in the desert for forty years. They didn't have the types of medicines we have today. They may not have known if certain diseases were contagious.

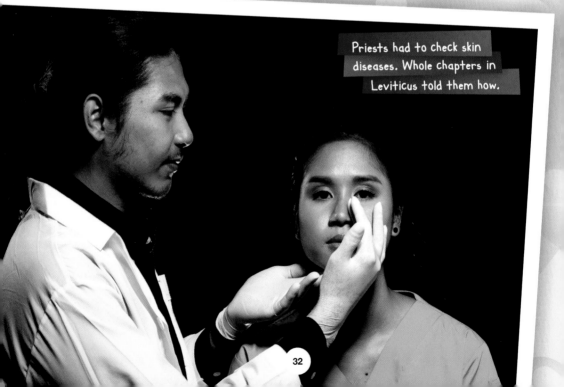

Priests had to check skin diseases. Whole chapters in Leviticus told them how.

FAST FACTS

Your skin is the **largest organ** in your body.

Skin has three main layers: the **epidermis**, **dermis**, and **subcutis**.

Your epidermis is thickest on your **palms** and the **soles** of your feet.

The **pigment melanin** determines the color of your skin.

Much of the dust in your house is **dead skin**.

Rules About Skin Diseases

Here's an example of what Leviticus says about skin disease:

"If there is in the skin of one's body a boil and it heals, and in the place of the boil there comes a white swelling or a reddish-white spot, then it shall be shown to the priest. And the priest shall look, and if it appears deeper than the skin and its hair has turned white, then the priest shall pronounce him unclean."
(Leviticus 13:18–20)

Whole chapters of Leviticus describe what priests should look for and how to respond to skin diseases. The book describes boils, scabs, rashes, burns, and things that ooze out of the body. It even tells what to do with clothing that touches icky skin diseases or mold.

Usually, a priest would look at the affected part of the skin. Then, the patient would be kept away from healthy people for seven days. After that time, the priest would check again. If the skin looked better, the patient was considered "clean" and could wash and return to the camp. However, if the skin was not better, the priest would declare the person "unclean." That meant he or she had to live outside the camp and have no contact with others. If anyone came near the sick person, the sick person had to shout, "Unclean, unclean."

A Very Serious "Time-Out"

Numbers 12

Being a big sister isn't always easy, especially if your little brother is one of God's greatest prophets. As sisters sometimes do, Miriam (the older sister of Moses who helped to save his life when he was an infant) said some mean things about her brother. The Bible tells us she got into big trouble for bad-mouthing Moses.

Miriam and Aaron, Moses's brother, were upset about who Moses had married. Irritated, they began to talk about Moses behind his back. They raised questions, asking whether God had only spoken through Moses or if God might speak through them also.

God did not allow Miriam and Aaron to talk about Moses in this way! He

Numbers 12 tells us that both of Moses's siblings, Miriam and Aaron, spoke against him, but only Miriam was punished.

34

called all three siblings to him. Then God appeared to them in a great cloud. God was angry at Aaron and Miriam for speaking against Moses. He reminded them that Moses was a special prophet, who spoke with God face to face. "Why then were you not afraid to speak against my servant Moses?" God asked Miriam and Aaron. Then God left, angry at Miriam and Aaron.

When the cloud cleared, something was different. Miriam's skin was as white as snow! Aaron could see that she had a terrible skin disease, making her unclean. He begged Moses not to punish them and not to let Miriam suffer from the terrible skin disease.

Moses called out to God to heal Miriam. God would do so, but first she spent seven days outside the camp. No one could go near her while her skin was unclean. After seven days, she could return, healed of her disease.

But That's Not Fair!

Numbers 12 tells us that both of Moses's siblings, Miriam and Aaron, spoke against him, but only Miriam was punished. Earlier in the Bible, Aaron caused major trouble by making a golden idol for the Israelites while Moses was away (Exodus 32). Numbers 20:24 shows that later, when Aaron did not believe God at the water of Meribah, he was not allowed to enter the land of Canaan.

did you KNOW?

The Bible often refers to skin diseases as "leprosy," but that can include many different things. Today, skin conditions have specific names, like acne, rosacea, eczema, hives—and leprosy. Doctors who treat the skin are called dermatologists.

Tumors and Mice

1 Samuel 4–6

What's your most prized possession? A special photo? A trophy? A quilt from your grandma? The Israelites had no trouble answering that question. It was the ark of the covenant, a wooden chest covered in gold. The ark of the covenant represented God's presence among the people. The book of Hebrews says the ark held a copy of the Ten Commandments that God gave to Moses, along with Aaron's staff and a pot of manna.

When the Philistine army attacked, things looked bad for the Israelites.

They were losing the battle and wanted a way to win. The elders decided to bring the ark of the covenant to the battlefield. This did not work. Besides that, the ark was stolen!

The Philistine victors put this special object in their temple to the god Dagon. The next morning, they found the statue of Dagon facedown on the ground before the ark. They set the statue upright again, but the next morning it was on the ground again.

The ark held special objects, including a copy of the Ten Commandments.

This time, its head and hands were broken off.

On top of that, the people of the Philistine city began to suffer from mysterious tumors. In a panic, they sent the ark to another city. However, the people of that city also broke out in tumors, so they sent the ark on to a third city. People there also broke out in tumors, and many people died.

Finally, after seven months, the Philistines decided to return the ark to the Israelites. Not only that, they also sent along an apology gift—five tumors and five mice, all made of gold.

The Bible doesn't tell us what the Israelites did with the gold tumors or mice. However, they were certainly thrilled to have their prized possession back.

did You KNOW?

- God gave Moses specific instructions about how the ark should be built (Exodus 25).
- The ark is connected to some miracles, such as the fall of the city walls of Jericho (Joshua 6).
- God struck dead a man named Uzzah for touching the ark (2 Samuel 6).
- No one knows where the ark ended up after the Babylonians destroyed Jerusalem, or where it is today.

More Bad News

At the time of this battle, Eli was the high priest in Israel. His two sons, Hophni and Phinehas, stayed near the ark of the covenant on the battlefield. However, they were killed (along with thirty thousand Israelites) when the Philistines captured the ark. When Eli heard about the death of his sons, he fell out of his chair, broke his neck, and died. Even Eli's daughter-in-law, Phinehas's wife, died that day, as she gave birth to a son.

Back from the Brink of Death

2 Kings 20:1–7

Normally, a boil is not a life-threatening problem. It's an infection that begins when a germ enters a hair follicle. It causes swelling, forming a bump filled with pus. It's definitely yucky, but not deadly. However, when the Bible mentions a boil, it often refers to something much more serious—as in the case of King Hezekiah.

Jerusalem was under attack, and the king was on his deathbed with a terrible illness. The prophet Isaiah came to visit. Sometimes, a visit from a prophet meant miraculous healing. However, this time Isaiah delivered bad news. "Set your house in order," he warned Hezekiah in 2 Kings 20:1, "for you shall die."

Hezekiah's boil might have been a sign of a serious illness, such as the plague. Hezekiah was beyond earthly healing. The king prayed to God. He even cried, calling on God to remember his faithfulness.

Isaiah ordered a mixture of figs to be placed on the king's boil. The king recovered from his illness

God heard Hezekiah's prayer and sent Isaiah back with good news. The prophet told the king God's message in 2 Kings 20:5: "I have heard your prayer. I will heal you." God also promised Hezekiah that he would defeat the Assyrians and live for fifteen more years. Then, Isaiah did something unusual. He ordered a mixture of figs to be placed on the king's boil. The king recovered from his illness.

AN UNUSUAL
SHADOW

King Hezekiah asked Isaiah for a sign that God would truly heal him. Isaiah asked, "Shall the shadow go forward ten steps, or go back ten steps?" (2 Kings 20:9). Hezekiah chose to have it move back ten steps, meaning the sun would move in a very unusual way in the sky. When Isaiah called out to God, the shadow moved back ten steps.

Fig Poultice

A *poultice* is a soft, moist, hot glob of plant material, such as herbs or oats. When placed on the body, it can help relieve soreness and swelling. Hezekiah's poultice was made from figs. Sometimes people might put herbs, grains, oil, or milk in a poultice.

Victory in Your Hands

Exodus 17:8–13

What does it take to win a great battle? A brave leader? Strong warriors? Sharp swords? The Israelites had all three, but their battle against the Amalekites was still a difficult one.

When the Amalekites attacked, Moses ordered Joshua to lead some men into battle. Surely Joshua was a great leader. Surely he chose the best warriors and they carried their best weapons. But this victory would depend on God.

Moses climbed a high hill over the battlefield. In his hands, he held the staff of God. He lifted the staff high as he raised his hands above the battle.

Aaron and Hur held Moses's arms up.

The Staff of God

Moses had been carrying this staff since the first time God spoke to him from a burning bush. On that day, the staff turned into a snake and back into a staff again (Exodus 4:1–4). It was also the same staff Moses held over the Red Sea to part the waters (Exodus 14:16, 21).

In this battle, as long as Moses held his hands high, the Israelites were winning. However, when Moses lowered his arms, the Amalekites would start winning. Eventually, Moses's hands grew tired. He could not hold them up any longer. What would happen to Joshua and the Israelites who were fighting the battle?

Thankfully, Moses was not alone on the hill. Aaron, Moses's brother, and Hur were there with him. They found a stone for Moses to sit on. Then they stood on either side of him and held his arms in the air. This way, Moses kept his hands raised the whole day, and the Israelites defeated the Amalekites.

WHO'S WHO?

Joshua was chosen by Moses to spy on Canaan and to lead the Israelite army. After Moses died, Joshua led the Israelites into the land of Canaan.

Aaron was Moses's brother and the first priest of Israel. He went with his brother to confront Pharaoh in Egypt. Aaron also used a staff to demonstrate God's power.

The Bible doesn't tell us much about Hur. According to some Jewish traditions, Hur was the son of Caleb, and when Moses was about to be taken by God, he appointed his nephew Hur, along with Aaron, as leader of the people.

A Secret Weapon

Joshua 6:1–21

The ancient city of Uruk (in modern-day Iraq) was one of the largest cities in the world five thousand years ago. It was surrounded by strong walls, built to protect the people from enemies. How do we know about Uruk's walls? Part of a wall is still standing today. The wall has survived thousands of years of floods, storms, and attacks.

Why, then, did the mighty wall around the city of Jericho fall down, all at once? What actually caused this incredible event that allowed Joshua to lead the Israelite army to victory?

Was it the marching? The Bible tells us that priests and warriors marched around the city of Jericho every day for a week. On the seventh day, they marched around the city seven times. But it wasn't the marching that brought down the walls.

Was it the trumpets or the shouting? We read in the book of Joshua that seven priests blew trumpets made of

The people of Israel followed God's instructions and the wall of Jericho fell.

rams' horns as they marched. On the seventh day, the trumpet blasts were followed by the Israelites' shouts. Seven trumpets and a huge crowd of shouting voices can be unbelievably loud, but they can't destroy stone walls.

Was it the ark of the covenant? The ark of the covenant represented God's presence. Inside the ark, according to the book of Hebrews, were a copy of the Ten Commandments, Aaron's staff, and other items.

The people inside the city of Jericho trusted their sturdy wall. They were so sure that the Israelites couldn't enter the city, they didn't even send out an army. The wall must have been strong indeed. What caused it to come tumbling down?

Meet Rahab

Why were Rahab and her family the only ones to survive the attack on Jericho? The story of how Rahab helped the Israelite spies who entered the city of Jericho, is told in Joshua 2. She hid the two spies in the roof of her home and then helped them escape through a window, which was built into the city wall. When the Israelite army attacked the city, they purposefully saved Rahab and her family (Joshua 6:17).

The book of Joshua says the Israelites followed God's instructions. "As soon as the people heard the sound of the trumpet, the people shouted a great shout, and the wall fell down flat, so that the people went up into the city, every man straight before him, and they captured the city" (Joshua 6:20).

Less Is More

Judges 7

From birds to bugs, frogs to fish, many animals can make themselves appear larger when threatened. Owls fluff their feathers. Puffer fish gulp water. Frilled lizards spread their skin. When these animals face an enemy, bigger is usually better.

In at least one case, the Bible tells a different story. The Israelite army of 32,000 was already the underdog as it prepared to face off against 135,000 Midianites. That's when God told Gideon his army was *too big*. God commanded Gideon to send home all the men who were afraid. The soldiers must have realized their chances of victory were slim, because 22,000 Israelites returned home. With only 10,000 men remaining, God once again showed Gideon how to determine who to send home. Gideon was left with only 300 men.

What was going on? God had already told Gideon that he would defeat the Midianites. This would not be because the Israelite army was bigger or better. Victory would come because the Israelites obeyed God.

$$
\begin{array}{r}
32{,}000 \\
-\ 22{,}000 \\
\hline
10{,}000 \\
-\ 9{,}700 \\
\hline
300
\end{array}
$$

When threatened, frilled lizards spread their skin to look bigger.

Not Just a Dream

Before the battle, God sent Gideon to spy on the Midianites. At the edge of camp, Gideon overheard an enemy soldier describe a dream. The Midianite said he saw a loaf of barley bread roll into camp and crush a tent. He believed the dream meant that Gideon would defeat them. The dream reassured Gideon he could win, even with a much smaller army.

The attack plan that God taught to Gideon would make his puny army seem huge. First, the Israelite army surrounded the Midianite camp at night. Then, at Gideon's signal, the soldiers all blew trumpets, smashed jars, and waved torches. This must have been a rude wake-up call for the Midianite army. They rushed out of their tents to find that they were surrounded by noise and lights. It probably seemed like a much larger army was attacking. Judges 7:22 says, "When they blew the 300 trumpets, the LORD set every man's sword against his comrade and against all the army." The Midianites began fighting one another!

did You KNOW?

The first time God reduced Gideon's army, he sent home all those who were afraid. The second time, he did something different. The soldiers stopped to drink from a stream. Almost all the men knelt down to drink. God told Gideon to send those men home. Only three hundred men used their hands to bring water up to their mouths. These were the soldiers Gideon brought into battle.

Solving a Giant Problem

1 Samuel 17

Have you ever witnessed bullying? It can be scary to deal with someone who taunts and threatens and picks fights. When that happens, you have options. You can ignore the bullying and hope it goes away. You can be a good friend to the person being bullied. You could go to an adult for help. Or sometimes, you can stand up to the bully.

Goliath mocked God and terrorized the Israelites. He was much taller than average, and he threatened the Israelite army every single day. When David, a young shepherd, showed up and witnessed this bullying, he made a decision.

David couldn't just ignore the taunting. He believed in God, and he believed God wanted the Israelites to win. Not only that, but David had already been chosen by God as the future king of Israel!

David couldn't comfort the people being terrorized. The Israelite army included warriors, a king, and David's own older brothers. They didn't want David's advice or friendship. In fact, David's brothers didn't want him there at all.

Could David go to an adult for help? All the bravest, strongest, most powerful adults were right there on the battlefield, shaking in their boots.

Few people expected David to defeat the giant.

FAST FACTS

125 pounds—the weight of Goliath's armor

15 pounds—the weight of Goliath's iron spearhead

did You KNOW?

Goliath isn't the only giant-like person mentioned in the Bible. According to Genesis 6:4, giants called Nephilim lived before the Flood. The Bible also mentions the Anakim and Rephaim (Deuteronomy 2:11, 20–21, 3:11; Joshua 12:4), also tall people groups. The Amorites' height was compared to cedars, or huge trees (Amos 2:9). The Israelites who spied on Canaan reported that the people there were "of great height" (Numbers 13:32). In a later battle, David's soldiers kill "a man of great stature, who had six fingers on each hand, and six toes on each foot" (2 Samuel 21:20).

With great faith in his God, David decided to stand up to Goliath. It was more than a long shot. It seemed downright impossible. David faced the giant Goliath with a sling and a few small rocks.

Goliath never bothered the Israelites, or anyone, again. David killed him with a single stone and then cut off his head.

One Against Many

1 Kings 18:16–40

There are many different ways to start a campfire. After piling up dry wood and kindling, you could use a match. You could make a spark by striking flint against steel. It's even possible to create enough friction by rubbing sticks together to start a fire. One thing that never works is dumping water all over the wood—unless you're the prophet Elijah.

Elijah challenged the prophets of Baal to a showdown.

Israel was in trouble. Evil King Ahab and the people had ignored their God. Instead, they worshiped the Canaanite god, Baal. It was time for the prophet Elijah to come out of hiding and challenge the prophets of Baal to a showdown.

This showdown was one against 450 as Elijah met the prophets of Baal on Mount Carmel. Many Israelites came to watch. Elijah set the ground rules for the prophets of Baal: "We'll each sacrifice a bull to put on the wood. Do not light a fire. Instead, call on your god to light the fire." The challenge was on.

The prophets of Baal built up their altar and sacrificed a bull. Then they called on Baal to light the fire. They begged, shouted, danced, and even cut themselves with swords. All day long they cried out to Baal, but there was no answer. Elijah teased them, suggesting that maybe their God was thinking, going to the bathroom, on vacation, or asleep.

Finally, Elijah built his own altar and sacrificed a bull. Before calling on his God, he ordered the people to fill four large jars with water and pour it over the wood. Two more times they filled the jars and soaked the wood. Then Elijah prayed, "Answer me, O LORD, answer me, that this people may know that you, O LORD, are God" (1 Kings 18:37).

The fire of Elijah's God fell on the altar. It burned up the bull, the wood, the stones, the soil, and even the puddles of water. The people "fell on their faces and said, 'The LORD, he is God' " (1 Kings 18:39).

Two Bad Apples

The Bible tells us that King Ahab "did evil in the eyes of the LORD, more than all who were before him" (1 Kings 16:30). However, his wife, Jezebel, was probably just as evil. They both worshiped other gods and turned the people of Israel away from God. Jezebel tried to kill every prophet of the Lord in Israel. Eventually Ahab was killed in battle and Jezebel was pushed from a window to her death.

A Wrestling Injury

Genesis 32:22–32

Isn't it fun to wrestle with your dad, brother, or cousins? Maybe they take it easy on you because you're smaller. The book of Genesis tells us that Jacob had an epic wrestling match. It didn't stop at bedtime, and his opponent did not go easy on him.

Jacob was on his way to meet his brother, Esau. Because they'd had problems in the past, Jacob didn't know whether his brother would hug him or kill him. But God told Jacob to go, so he obeyed. Jacob sent ahead some servants with gifts for Esau. Then he sent his family across a stream. The rest of his servants carried all of Jacob's possessions across the stream. Jacob was left alone, or so he thought.

The book of Genesis tells us that Jacob had an epic wrestling match.

A Nasty Trick

When Jacob and Esau were younger, Jacob deceived Isaac, their father. As the older brother, Esau had the right to his father's blessing. But Jacob was his mother's favorite, and she came up with a plan to steal Esau's blessing. While Esau was out hunting, Jacob put on a disguise. He wore Esau's clothes and some goat skins to make himself seem hairy, like Esau. His mother, Rebekah, prepared delicious food for Jacob to give to Isaac. Jacob's blind father was fooled, and he gave Esau's blessing to Jacob.

The next thing he knew, Jacob was wrestling with another man! The two men wrestled all night until the sun came up. The mysterious man could not overpower Jacob. He touched Jacob's hip, causing a serious injury and proving his power. But still Jacob held on. "Let me go," the man said, "for the day has broken."

Even with an injured hip, Jacob did not let the man go. "I will not let you go unless you bless me," Jacob said.

Finally, the two stopped wrestling. The man changed Jacob's name to Israel and gave him a blessing. He did not tell Israel his own name. Who was this man? Was it an angel? Was it God?

did You KNOW?

After Jacob's wrestling match, he named the place Peniel. It means "face of God." Jacob's own name has an important meaning: "he grasps the heel." When Jacob was born, he was grasping his twin brother's heel. However, the name can also mean "he deceives," which describes Jacob's behavior well. After the wrestling match, Jacob's name changed to Israel, which means "he struggles with God."

When the wrestling match ended and the man had gone, Jacob said, "I have seen God face to face, and yet my life has been delivered." Then he limped off to meet up with his family.

51

Samson's Revenge

Judges 15

Samson was a man with superhero-like strength. But he didn't always use his strength well. After his Philistine wife betrayed him at their wedding (see *A Strange Container for Honey* on p. 22), Samson abandoned her. After he lost a bet, he beat up thirty men to take their clothes as payment for the bet.

Now Samson was mad again. He had gone to see his wife (the one he had abandoned) but was stopped by her father. She was married to someone else now. Samson was so angry that he wanted to hurt all the Philistines, so he came up with a plan.

Samson captured three hundred wild foxes. This amazing feat must have taken some time. The whole time, Samson stayed angry and plotted revenge. He tied the foxes together by their tails in pairs. Then he attached a torch to each pair of tails. Samson lit the torches and set the foxes loose in the fields of the Philistines. This created a disaster. Fire burned up all the grain, the grapes, and the olive trees.

The Philistines were so upset, they killed Samson's wife and her father. Of course, this made Samson even angrier. He attacked the Philistines, killing many. Later, when the Philistines came looking for Samson, he attacked again. This time, his only weapon was the jawbone of a dead donkey. He used it to kill a thousand men.

Samson captured three hundred wild foxes and tied them together in pairs by their tails.

What Does the Bible Say about Revenge?

The book of Judges shows how Samson attacked his enemies. Other books in the Bible offer different ways to deal with enemies:

- "If your enemy is hungry, give him bread to eat, and if he is thirsty, give him water to drink" (Proverbs 25:21).

- Numbers 35 gives ways for taking revenge lawfully.

- "Love your enemies and pray for those who persecute you" (Matthew 5:44).

- Romans 12:17 says, "Repay no one evil for evil, but give thought to do what is honorable in the sight of all."

SUPER STRENGTH

After his first attack on the Philistines, Samson hid in a cave near Judah. The people of Judah were afraid. They said to Samson, "We have come down to bind you, that we may give you into the hands of the Philistines" (Judges 15:11). Samson let the people of Judah tie him up. They brought Samson out of the cave and gave him to the Philistines. Then, according to Judges 15:14, "the Spirit of the LORD rushed upon" Samson and he broke the ropes. That's when he attacked the Philistines with the jawbone.

A Little Privacy, Please?

1 Samuel 24

Things were not going well between David and his father-in-law, King Saul. In fact, King Saul was determined to kill David. He led three thousand soldiers in search of David in the wilderness. Where could David be hiding?

While searching near a place called the Wildgoats' Rocks, Saul needed to go to the bathroom. Since there were no public bathrooms in the wilderness, the king ducked into a cave for some privacy. However, he was not alone in the cave.

King Saul didn't know it, but David and his men were hiding in the back of that very cave. While Saul relieved himself, David crept through the darkness. He snuck up behind Saul and quietly pulled out a knife. What do you think he did next?

David's men wanted him to kill Saul and become king himself, but David knew that God had anointed Saul as king. Instead, David gently cut some fabric from Saul's robe and snuck away. Saul never even knew he was there. Once Saul had finished, he left the cave.

Since there were no public bathrooms, King Saul ducked into a cave.

David's Rise to King

As a young shepherd boy, David was visited by the prophet Samuel. God had told Samuel to anoint David king of Israel. A short time later, David began to work for King Saul as a lyre player and armor-bearer. Eventually, David married the king's daughter and became best friends with the king's son Jonathan. David led King Saul's armies to many victories and was well loved by the Israelites. He became king when he was thirty years old.

That's when David appeared and called out to him. He showed Saul that he had been close enough to cut off the corner of his robe but did not kill him. He assured Saul he would not lay a hand on him, that he was not Saul's enemy.

Saul recognized David and said, "I know that you shall surely be king." Saul asked David to never wipe out his children or grandchildren. David promised not to hurt Saul or his descendants. Sure enough, when Saul later died in battle, David became king and kept his promise.

Dirty Laundry

Jeremiah 13:1–11

What's under your bed? A neat stack of board games? A pile of dirty laundry? What if your mom dug out a pair of underwear so old and stinky they had to be thrown away? Sounds gross, but it would probably get your attention! Believe it or not, God used an old pair of underwear to get the attention of the Israelites.

God commanded the prophet Jeremiah to buy a new pair of underwear. Some Bibles call it a "loincloth" or a "linen belt" or a "linen girdle," but make no mistake: it was underwear. God told Jeremiah to wear the underwear and never let it get wet. That meant no washing it or even swimming in it.

How long did Jeremiah have to keep wearing the same pair of unwashed underwear? The Bible doesn't tell us, but he wore it until God spoke to Jeremiah a second time. This time, God commanded Jeremiah to hide the underwear under a rock. Jeremiah obeyed. He probably hoped he would never see that underwear again!

Bible names for underwear include "loincloth," a "linen belt," or a "linen girdle."

More Discomfort for Jeremiah

The book of Jeremiah tells us that God gave the prophet another uncomfortable item to wear. Jeremiah had to make a yoke out of wood. (A yoke is usually used to hold two animals together so they can pull a plow or wagon.) Jeremiah wore the yoke while he warned the Israelites about the future. Jeremiah wore it on his neck to demonstrate how God would put the Israelites under the heavy yoke of the Babylonian king Nebuchadnezzar (Jeremiah 27).

did You KNOW?

Before Jeremiah was born, God chose him to become a prophet. When God first spoke to him, Jeremiah worried that he was too young to know how to give God's messages to people. It was a difficult time in Israel's history. Jeremiah spoke mostly about God's judgment and told the Israelites to stop sinning. He is sometimes called "the weeping prophet" because he cried for Israel.

But God had other plans. Some time later, God told Jeremiah to go get the underwear he had hidden. Jeremiah did so. What he found was a ruined piece of clothing that was completely useless.

What was this crazy situation all about? God taught the people of Israel a lesson. They hadn't been listening to God, and now they were useless, like stinky old underwear. In the Bible, God communicates with people in many different ways, but you can bet the example of the underwear really got their attention!

LAUNDRY LIST

- An average American family does eight to ten loads of laundry per week.
- Laundry accounts for about one-fifth of the water used inside a home.
- A washing machine requires about thirteen gallons of water to do one load of laundry.

A Haircut Full of Meaning

Ezekiel 5

Jerusalem was in trouble. As they had in the past, the people had turned away from God to worship idols. So, once again, God sent a prophet with a stern warning. This time, God used a haircut to show the people of Jerusalem their future.

God told the prophet Ezekiel to cut off all his hair and his whole beard. This wasn't just a trim. It represented the full destruction of Jerusalem. Did Ezekiel use a razor or a knife to cut his hair? No, he used a sharp sword to represent God's judgment.

God then instructed Ezekiel to carefully weigh the cut hair and split it into three equal piles. Ezekiel burned the first pile inside the city walls. This represented the people who would die of illness and starvation in Jerusalem. Ezekiel took the second pile outside the city and struck it with a sword. This represented those who would die by the sword outside the city. Ezekiel let the third pile blow away in the wind. It represented the people God would scatter to the winds.

According to God's instructions, Ezekiel kept a small bit of his hair tucked in his robe. Then he threw those hairs into the fire as well.

God instructed Ezekiel to split his hair into three equal piles: one for people who would die in Jerusalem, one for those who would die outside the city, and one for people God would scatter to the winds.

Who Was Ezekiel?

Ezekiel was a prophet when the Israelites were captives in Babylon. He first preached messages of judgment and repentance. Then, in captivity, he preached hope that Jerusalem would be restored. Ezekiel's haircut wasn't his only unusual experience. The book of Ezekiel says he had a vision in which he ate a scroll (see *Feasting on God's Words* on p. 26) and ate barley cakes cooked over manure (see *No Bread for Me, Thanks* on p. 28). Ezekiel's name means "may God strengthen him."

HAIR-RAISING FACTS

- Hair is the fastest-growing tissue in the human body other than bone marrow.
- Hair can stretch 30% longer when it's wet.
- A single hair is strong enough to support one hundred grams, or about the weight of a bar of soap.
- Hair is made of keratin, the same protein that forms horns, hooves, beaks, and claws in animals.

From Palace to Pasture

Daniel 4

insane
/inˈsān/
adjective mentally sick; in an abnormal state of mind

King Nebuchadnezzar seemed to have it all. He was rich and powerful. He ruled over Babylon from a beautiful palace. The problem was that Nebuchadnezzar took credit for it all instead of honoring God.

One day, Nebuchadnezzar stood on the roof of his palace admiring his kingdom. He said to himself, "Is not this great Babylon, which I have built by my mighty power . . . and for the glory of my majesty?" (Daniel 4:30). God did not approve of that boasting! In fact, God had warned Nebuchadnezzar about his pride one year earlier in a dream.

Now it was time for the proud king to learn who was really in charge. As soon as Nebuchadnezzar finished speaking, God told him, "The kingdom has departed from you, and your dwelling shall be with the beasts of the field. And you shall be made to eat grass like an ox . . . until you know that the Most High rules the kingdom of men" (Daniel 4:31–32). Nebuchadnezzar became insane, living alone in the wild. His hair and nails grew long and unruly. He ate grass like an ox. His body was soaked with dew. This humbled the once-great king.

Nebuchadnezzar became insane after pridefully taking credit for his wealth and power.

Nebuchadnezzar spent seven years out of his mind. Then, finally, when he looked toward heaven and proclaimed Daniel's God to be supreme, he acted with reason again.

The king regained not only his mind but also his kingdom. He became even greater than before. This time, however, he gave God the glory.

NEBUCHADNEZZAR IN ARCHAEOLOGY

In 1803, archaeologists found a stone tablet among the ruins of Babylon. It contains ancient writing about Nebuchadnezzar and the other gods he once worshiped. An excerpt reads, "I am Nebuchadnezzar, king of Babylon, the exalted prince, the favorite of the god marduk, the beloved of the god Nabu." The tablet is known as the East India House Inscription.

Nebuchadnezzar's Dream

One year before going insane, Nebuchadnezzar had a prophetic dream. He saw an enormous tree. It grew fruit and sheltered animals. People could see the tree from all over the world. Then, in the dream, a heavenly messenger commanded that the branches be cut off. The fruit was scattered, and the animals ran away. Only the stump remained. Daniel, the king's advisor, understood the meaning of the dream. He begged Nebuchadnezzar to turn from his sin and acknowledge God, but the king didn't listen.

Heavenly Security Guards

Genesis 3:24; Ezekiel 1, 10

The very first humans had messed up. God had given Adam and Eve one rule, and they broke it. God sent them away from the garden of Eden forever. God placed cherubim and a flaming sword at the entrance of the garden to guard the tree of life.

> If you're picturing cute, rosy-cheeked, naked babies with wings, think again.

If you're picturing cute, rosy-cheeked, naked babies with wings, think again. Cherubim are far from the angel babies often shown in artwork. So what are cherubim? What do they look like? Where do they come from?

Cherubim (plural for *cherub*, which may be a type of angel) appear for the first time in the Bible in the garden of Eden, but they show up in other places throughout the Bible. Our best descriptions of cherubim come from two visions. In the first, the prophet Ezekiel saw four living creatures that were bright, like lightning, and flying around the throne of God. They seemed to have human bodies, but instead of one face, they each had four! One face looked human, but the other three looked like a lion, an ox, and an eagle. Each cherub also had four wings; two wings stretched up and two covered its body. Ezekiel also describes wheels that moved with the cherubim. The wheels were covered in eyes. We can

did You KNOW?

- The Bible mentions many types of spiritual beings, including cherubim, seraphim, angels, and demons.
- Angels are mentioned almost three hundred times in the Bible.
- Some angels in the Bible appear like human men.
- Cherubim and seraphim have wings, but the Bible doesn't say if all angels have wings.
- In the Bible, angels have many jobs: they worship God, bring destruction, give God's messages, warn people of danger, blind people, protect people, rescue people, and help people.
- The only angels named in the Bible are Michael and Gabriel.

SING ALONG

The book of Revelation in the New Testament says that the living creatures constantly repeated these words:

Holy, holy, holy,
is the Lord God Almighty,
who was and is and is to come!

only imagine that this vision of heaven was hard for Ezekiel to put into words!

The New Testament contains the book called Revelation. This book's author (John) also saw similar creatures in his vision of heaven. We don't know for certain that these were cherubim, but he saw figures like a lion, an ox, a man, and an eagle. They had six wings and were covered in eyes. In heaven, they sang God's praises every day and

every night. According to John, the voice of one of these creatures sounded like thunder.

Other sections of the Bible describe cherubim used as decorations. Cherubim of gold, wood, and woven cloth decorated the tabernacle, the temple, and the ark of the covenant. How did the craftsmen know what these beings looked like?

A Sign in the Skies

Genesis 9:8–17

You've probably noticed married adults wearing wedding rings. The ring is a symbol of the promises they've made to each other. God also uses a symbol to represent his promise, but he didn't choose jewelry. Instead, he chose to make a rainbow appear in the sky.

According to a story in Genesis, people became very wicked. In fact, they were so wicked, God had to destroy most of his creation and start over. You might know about Noah's ark. When the flood ended, God made a promise to Noah and "to every living creature." He said, "The waters shall never again become a flood to destroy all flesh" (Genesis 9:15).

This very serious promise, or covenant, was marked by a symbol—a rainbow. It would remind God and people that God would not flood the whole earth again.

A rainbow appears when water droplets in the sky (rain or mist) bend light rays.

Biblical Rainbows

In the prophet Ezekiel's vision, he describes God's glory as appearing like a rainbow (Ezekiel 1:28). The New Testament tells of John's vision of heaven, which also describes rainbows. One forms a circle around God's throne (Revelation 4:3). Another appears above the head of an angel (Revelation 10:1).

The Science Behind Rainbows

A rainbow appears when water droplets in the sky (rain or mist) bend light rays. To see a rainbow, you must stand with the sun behind you. Although you'll see an arc or part of an arc, a rainbow is actually a full circle. It always appears with red at the top of the arc and violet at the bottom (or inside). Sometimes, moonlight forms a "moonbow." It's not as bright as a rainbow because the light is weaker, since it's sunlight reflected off the moon.

A FUNNY NAME

You can remember the seven colors of a rainbow from top to bottom by thinking of the name *Roy G. Biv*:

Red
Orange
Yellow
Green
Blue
Indigo
Violet

The Burning Bush

Exodus 3, 4:1–17

"Take your sandals off your feet, for the place on which you are standing is holy ground." With these words, God began a conversation with Moses in Exodus 3:5.

Moses was working as a shepherd in the wilderness. He might have spent many days alone with no one to talk to and nothing new to see. After forty years of this quiet life, Moses was in for a big surprise.

Moses saw a bush that looked like it was on fire, but it never burned up. This rare sight caught his attention.

Moses asked God, "What should I tell them?"

Fire in the Bible

The burning bush isn't the only time God used fire. Here are some others:

- A pillar of fire led the Israelites in the wilderness (see *A Pillar of Cloud and Fire* on p. 68).
- A blazing torch appeared when God made a covenant with Abram (Genesis 15:17).
- God came down to Mount Sinai in fire (Exodus 19:18).
- God sent fire to light Elijah's sacrifice (see *One Against Many* on p. 48).

NAMES OF GOD

The Bible records many different names for God. The Israelites called him God Almighty (*El Shaddai*), The Most High God (*El Elyon*), and The Everlasting God (*El Olam*). They also used The Lord My Shepherd (*Jehovah-Raah*) and The Lord Will Provide (*Jehovah Jireh*). The Israelites used over fifteen different names for God.

Once Moses was paying full attention, God said to him: "I am the God of your father, the God of Abraham, the God of Isaac, and the God of Jacob" (Exodus 3:6). Then God said, "I will send you to Pharaoh that you may bring my people, the children of Israel, out of Egypt" (Exodus 3:10). He gave Moses signs to show the people that he truly was God. First, Moses's staff turned into a snake and back into a staff again. Then Moses's hand turned as white as snow with a skin disease and was healed again.

Moses asked God in Exodus 3:13–14 what he should say to the people if they asked for God's name: "What should I tell them?"

God answered Moses, "I AM."

After that day in front of the burning bush, God spoke to Moses many times. Through direct instructions to Moses, God guided the Israelites out of slavery and through the wilderness. God showed the people how to live and how to treat one another.

A Pillar of Cloud and Fire

Exodus 13:5, 21–22, 14:19–30

How do you picture a perfect paradise? A warm beach? A breezy field? For the Israelites, the perfect paradise God promised them was "a land flowing with milk and honey" (Exodus 13:5).

Before the Israelites entered the land, they wandered in the wilderness for forty years. During those forty years, it was cold and dark at night. It was hot and sunny during the day. The food was boring (see *The Same Breakfast for Forty Years* on p. 20).

During the day, God went before them as a pillar of cloud that showed them the way to go. At night, God went before them as a pillar of fire that gave them light.

God promised the Israelites "a land flowing with milk and honey."

God's pillar even protected the Israelites. When the angry Egyptians chased them, the pillar of cloud moved behind the fleeing Israelites. There, it stood between them and the Egyptian army. It brought darkness on the Egyptians and kept them away from the Israelites. God looked down from the pillar and threw the enemy army into confusion. This allowed the Israelites to escape across the Red Sea. Eventually, this pillar of cloud and fire led the Israelites to the land of Canaan.

Cloud Sightings

The book of Revelation in the New Testament mentions several clouds:

- According to the author of Revelation, when Jesus comes "with the clouds . . . every eye will see him" (1:5–7).
- An angel comes down from heaven "wrapped in a cloud" (10:1).
- Two prophets go "up to heaven in a cloud" while "their enemies watched them" (11:12).
- A man with a golden crown on his head sits on a "white cloud" (14:14).

God in a Cloud

The pillar of cloud isn't the only time God appeared in a cloud. Here are some others:

- God spoke to Moses from within a cloud that covered Mount Sinai for six days (Exodus 24:15–18).
- God appeared in a cloud over the mercy seat in the tabernacle (Leviticus 16:2).
- God's glory appeared in a cloud covering the tent of meeting (Numbers 16:42).
- God's glory filled the temple in the form of a cloud (1 Kings 8:10–11).

Chariots of Fire

2 Kings 6:8–23

God's chosen prophets could do some pretty amazing things. At times, they could hear, understand, and do things that other people could not. Sometimes, prophets could even see things others could not see. That was the case with Elisha.

The king of Syria wanted to capture the prophet Elisha. He sent soldiers with horses and chariots to Elisha's city of Dothan. Early in the morning, Elisha's servant went out and saw that they were surrounded. He started to panic. "What shall we do?" he cried.

Elisha did not panic. He could also see something the servant couldn't see. "Do not be afraid," he told his servant, "for those who are with us are more than those who are with them" (2 Kings 6:16). What was Elisha talking about? At that moment, he prayed that his servant would see what he saw. God opened the servant's eyes. Suddenly, the servant could see a huge army of horses and chariots of fire surrounding and protecting Elisha!

God's prophets could sometimes hear, understand, and do things that other people could not.

did You KNOW?

The prophet Elijah never died. Instead, he was taken up into heaven, right in front of Elisha's eyes. When that happened, chariots of fire and horses of fire appeared (2 Kings 2:11).

God struck the Syrian army with blindness. The soldiers could not see where they were going. They must have been confused as well, because they obeyed Elisha when he said, "This is not the way, and this is not the city. Follow me, and I will bring you to the man whom you seek" (2 Kings 6:19).

Elisha led the enemy army to Samaria. There, he prayed that the eyes of the Syrian soldiers would be opened again. The Syrian soldiers could now see they were in trouble. Would they be killed? No. Elisha told the king of Israel to give the soldiers food and water and then release them. The Syrians returned home.

Blindness in the Bible

The Syrian soldiers weren't the only ones God struck blind in the Bible. Here are some other examples:

- Angels struck the men of Sodom blind when they tried to get into Lot's house (Genesis 19:11).

- Saul was surrounded by a bright light, heard a voice from heaven, and lost his sight for a time (Acts 9:3–9).

- A false prophet and sorcerer named Bar-Jesus became temporarily blind (Acts 13:11).

Is It Warm in Here?

Daniel 1, 3

Shadrach, Meshach, and Abednego were Jewish captives in Babylon. The three young men worked hard and served Nebuchadnezzar, the Babylonian king. But they also served and obeyed God. One day, they had to make a hard choice between the two.

King Nebuchadnezzar had built a ninety-foot-tall golden statue. He commanded all people to fall down and worship the statue when they heard music play. Those who didn't obey would be thrown into a fiery furnace and killed. Shadrach, Meshach, and Abednego knew the rule and the punishment. But when the music played, they didn't bow down. They believed it was wrong to worship anything besides their God.

Three men went inside the furnace. But then there were four men, and each was perfectly fine!

Working for the King

When the Babylonians defeated Jerusalem, King Nebuchadnezzar took many treasures, including some smart young men. Daniel, Shadrach, Meshach, and Abednego lived and trained in the king's palace. The king gave them new Babylonian names. They learned the Babylonian language and became advisors to the king. But they always obeyed their God first.

Hebrew Name	Babylonian Name
Daniel	Belteshazzar
Hananiah	Shadrach
Mishael	Meshach
Azariah	Abednego

King Nebuchadnezzar became very angry. He ordered the furnace to be heated seven times hotter than usual. He had his strongest guards tie up Shadrach, Meshach, and Abednego and throw them in the furnace. The furnace was so hot that the guards who threw them in died in the flames!

But something strange happened. Inside the furnace, there weren't three dying men. There were four men, and they were perfectly fine! They weren't tied up, and they weren't harmed. King Nebuchadnezzar could see with his own eyes that one looked "like a son of the gods" (Daniel 3:25).

Who was the fourth man? Was it an angel? The astonished king called Shadrach, Meshach, and Abednego out of the furnace. The three men did not have a single scorch mark on their clothes. They didn't even smell like smoke. Nebuchadnezzar praised God and cried, "Blessed be the God of Shadrach, Meshach, and Abednego, who has sent his angel and delivered his servants, who trusted in him" (Daniel 3:28).

From that day on, King Nebuchadnezzar made it illegal to say anything bad against the God of Shadrach, Meshach, and Abednego. He also gave the three young men important jobs in his kingdom.

Fingers Floating Free

Daniel 5

Maybe you've heard the saying "The writing's on the wall." It means that the truth has become clear and it's bad news. The saying comes from an event recorded in the Bible—an event that has a creepy twist!

One night, during a big party, King Belshazzar called for the gold cups that had been stolen from God's temple in Jerusalem. The party guests drank from the cups and praised the gods of gold, bronze, iron, wood, and stone.

Just then, something very strange happened that shocked them all. The fingers of a human hand appeared and wrote on the wall. There was no head, no body—just a mysterious hand. It wrote a message on the wall that no one could understand. King Belshazzar was so terrified his knees started knocking together.

Mysteriously, the fingers of a human hand appeared and wrote on the wall. There was no head, no body—just a hand.

Like Father, Like Son

The book of Daniel shows how King Nebuchadnezzar acted pridefully when he was king (see *From Palace to Pasture* on p. 60 and *Is It Warm in Here?* on p. 72). Now, his son Belshazzar was king, and he was repeating some of his father's prideful ways. Both kings disobeyed God by worshiping other things. Daniel told Belshazzar that when Nebuchadnezzar's heart became full of pride, God took him off his throne. Then Daniel said, "And you his son, Belshazzar, have not humbled your heart, though you knew all this" (Daniel 5:22).

He asked wise men and magicians to read the words, but they couldn't. He offered great rewards to anyone who could tell him the meaning, but no one could do it. Finally, the queen reminded King Belshazzar that a man named Daniel, who had helped the king's father, could understand dreams and riddles. So Daniel was brought before the king.

Sure enough, Daniel could read the message. The words that were written on the wall—*Mene, Mene, Tekel, Parsin*—were bad news. They meant that King Belshazzar's kingdom was coming to an end. His kingdom would be given to an enemy. Daniel received great honors for reading the message, but the king was killed that very night. An enemy took over his kingdom.

Daniel's Helper

Daniel 8:1–18, 9:20–27

When you don't understand something, do you ask your parents? A teacher? An older brother or sister? In the Bible, a man named Daniel had some visions he didn't understand. But his parents and teachers couldn't help him. God sent a special messenger named Gabriel to help Daniel.

Gabriel, an angel, is mentioned in other books of the Bible, including the Gospel of Luke (1:19). In this story, he explained a vision to Daniel. This vision included a powerful ram with lopsided horns. It fought with an even more powerful goat with one horn between his eyes. Later, the goat's horn broke and four horns appeared in its place. This might seem like just a weird dream, but it was full of meaning.

Daniel was very afraid. He fell to the ground with his face down. Gabriel explained to Daniel that the animals and horns represented nations and kings. Daniel was seeing the future in his vision. After hearing about his vision, Daniel was sick for days.

Daniel's helper, the angel Gabriel, is mentioned in other places in the Bible, including Luke 1:19.

Later, Gabriel appeared to Daniel again. This time, Daniel was praying for the people of Israel. He tried to understand when they would be able to return to their own land. Gabriel appeared "in swift flight" and encouraged Daniel. He said, "O Daniel, I have now come out to give you insight and understanding . . . for you are greatly loved" (Daniel 9:22–23). Many Bible teachers believe that Gabriel told Daniel that Jerusalem and the temple would eventually be rebuilt.

Your Son Is Alive!

1 Kings 17:8–24

The Bible describes many amazing miracles. The first story in the Bible about someone being raised from the dead is found in the book of 1 Kings.

God had commanded Elijah to go to a town called Zarephath. God told a widow there to feed Elijah. She was poor and almost starving until a miracle caused her to have plenty of food. She shared it with Elijah. One day her son became ill. As the days passed, his illness became worse and worse. The boy stopped breathing and died.

The widow did not ask Elijah to bring her son back to life. Instead, she accused Elijah of going to her house to cause her son to die. She was sad and angry.

First Kings 17 in the Bible is packed with wild and wacky happenings!

One Miracle After Another

First Kings 17 is one chapter of the Bible that's packed with wild and wacky happenings! Check out these amazing events from this time in Elijah's life:

- Elijah tells King Ahab that there would be no rain or dew in the land.
- Ravens feed Elijah in the wilderness (see *Ravens That Deliver Dinner* on p. 14).
- The widow's containers don't run out of flour or oil during the drought.

Elijah carried the boy upstairs and placed him on a bed. Then Elijah stretched out over the dead boy three times and prayed, "O LORD my God, let this child's life come into him again." God listened to Elijah's prayer. The boy came back to life!

Elijah brought the boy downstairs to his mother. "See, your son lives," he said to the widow.

The widow said to Elijah, "Now I know that you are a man of God."

Great Teacher, God's Power

2 Kings 4:8–37

Pay attention in class or you might miss something important. Elisha was a good student who learned from a great teacher—the prophet Elijah. It's possible that Elijah told his student about how he prayed for God to raise a boy from the dead. And that lesson may have come in handy when Elisha needed to do the same thing.

Elisha wanted to show kindness to his friend, a woman who lived in a town called Shunem. She and her husband had made a room for Elisha in their home. They always welcomed him. What could he give them in return? They had many good things: a nice home, plenty of food, and lots of money. But they had no son.

Elisha told the woman that by this time next year, she would have a son. She had a hard time believing Elisha's prophecy, but it came true. One year later, she had a son.

Elisha was a good student who learned from the prophet Elijah.

80

Similar Miracles

Elijah performed many miracles during his lifetime. One miracle involved a jar of flour and a jug of oil that didn't run out (1 Kings 17:8–16). Elisha performed a similar miracle. A widow came to him saying that her husband had died and she could not pay their debts. All she had was a small jar of oil. Elisha told her to gather every empty container she could find. She poured the oil from her small jar into the containers, and every container filled with oil. Then she was able to sell the oil to pay off the money she owed (2 Kings 4:1–7).

Years later, the boy had a sudden pain in his head. Something was terribly wrong. His mother held him in her lap. She wanted her little boy to get better, but he died. She put her dead son on Elisha's bed and then went to find the prophet.

The woman fell to the ground and grabbed Elisha's feet. He knew right away that something was very wrong. Elisha wanted to help her. He gave his staff to a servant and instructed him to lay the staff on the boy's face. The servant did so, but nothing happened. The boy was still dead.

When Elisha got to the house, he did just what his teacher, Elijah, had done in the same situation. First, he prayed. Then, he stretched his body out over the dead boy. Would it work? Would God bring the boy back to life? The boy started to feel warm. Elisha waited. He walked around the room. Then he stretched out over the boy a second time.

Suddenly, a sneeze! And another sneeze! After seven sneezes, the boy returned to life! Elisha's servant called the boy's mother to see her son.

A Quick Decision

2 Kings 13:14, 20–21

Imagine some men, far outside their city. They're sad because their friend has died. They're probably tired because they've carried him a long way. They might even be dirty from digging a grave. Suddenly, the sad, tired, dirty men notice something off in the distance. It's the enemy coming to attack!

They must make a quick decision. What should they do with their friend's body? They can't run back to the city carrying the dead man. It would be a disgrace to leave him lying out in the open. They don't have time to finish digging.

The book of 2 Kings tells us the prophet Elisha had grown old, gotten

Some people threw a dead man's body into Elisha's grave. The body touched Elisha's bones and came back to life!

did you KNOW?

Israelites had certain customs to mourn the deaths of their loved ones. They would wear special clothing made of sackcloth. They would also sit on the ground and pour dirt or ashes over their heads. Sometimes mourners would fast, which means to go without eating or drinking.

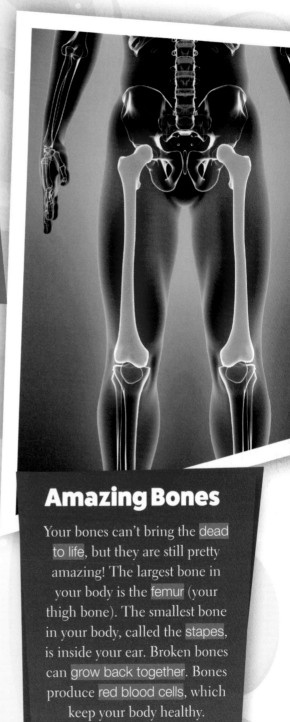

sick, and died. His body was buried in a grave. Later, some people were about to bury a man who had died. But they saw some enemies coming, so they threw the dead man's body into Elisha's grave. That's when a miracle happened: The body touched Elisha's bones and came back to life! The man stood on his feet and lived.

The formerly dead man might have been confused about where he was and what was going on. Were his friends there to see the miracle? Or had they already run away? The Bible doesn't tell us those answers. But the man was dead and now he was alive again.

Maybe others tried to lay their loved ones in Elisha's grave. Maybe they thought the bones would bring them a miracle. But the Bible only records this one time that someone was brought back to life by touching a prophet's bones.

Amazing Bones

Your bones can't bring the dead to life, but they are still pretty amazing! The largest bone in your body is the femur (your thigh bone). The smallest bone in your body, called the stapes, is inside your ear. Broken bones can grow back together. Bones produce red blood cells, which keep your body healthy.

Dry Bones

Ezekiel 37:1–14

You have 206 bones in your body! That might sound like a lot, but it's nothing compared to the number of bones Ezekiel saw in a vision. In his vision, Ezekiel was in a valley filled with bones. Everywhere he looked, bones were piled on top of bones.

God asked Ezekiel, "Can these bones live?"

Normally, the answer would be no. The bones were completely bare and dry. But Ezekiel answered, "O Lord GOD, you know." Then God commanded Ezekiel to prophesy over the dry bones.

First, there was a rattling sound. The bones were moving! They stacked one on top of another—the knee bone connected to the thigh bone, the thigh bone connected to the hip bone, and so on—but they were still dead, dry bones.

As Ezekiel continued to speak the words God told him to say, flesh appeared. The bones became covered in muscles and skin. But they still weren't alive.

God commanded Ezekiel to prophesy over the dry bones. First came a rattling sound. Then the bones stacked up!

As Ezekiel kept prophesying, breath came into the bodies. They stood up. They were alive! The valley was filled with living, breathing people where there were once only dry bones. The book of Ezekiel says they formed a "great army."

God explained the vision to Ezekiel. He told him that the bones are the people of Israel. Their hope had been lost. But God would put his spirit into the people and bring them to their own land.

Calling All Artists!

Illustrate the story of Ezekiel in the valley of dry bones. Make your picture more interesting by using dry pasta for bones. Glue different shapes of pasta to the paper. You can even form some into skeletons like the bones that connected in the story of Ezekiel.

SING ALONG

A song came out in the 1920s by James Weldon Johnson based on the story of Ezekiel and the dry bones. You can search "Dem Bones" (or "Dry Bones") online and sing along!

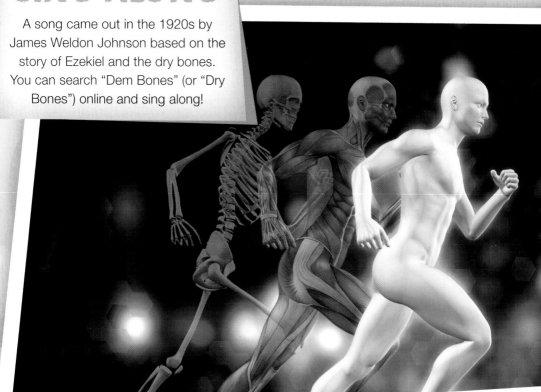

No Swimming

Exodus 7:14–24

The Nile River is one of the longest rivers in the world. It flows from the middle of Africa north to Egypt. The people of Egypt see the river as an important part of their lives. In ancient times people depended on the Nile to survive. So it's no surprise that the Nile River shows up in stories in the Bible.

Moses and Aaron met Pharaoh on his way to the river one morning. "The LORD, the God of the Hebrews, sent me to you, saying, 'Let my people go,'" Moses said to Pharaoh.

Then to show Pharaoh God's power, Aaron raised his staff and struck the water of the Nile. Suddenly, the fresh, clean water turned to blood. Red blood choked the fish and stunk up the air. If Pharaoh had planned on a morning swim that day, his plans would have surely been canceled.

In ancient times people depended on the Nile to survive. The river provided water, fish, transportation, and farming soil.

The Mighty Nile

People have lived near the Nile River in Egypt for thousands of years. The river provides people with water, fish, transportation, and good soil for farming. Before the Aswan High Dam was completed in 1970, the Nile would flood each year. The floodwater dumped rich, black soil on the dry land.

THE TEN PLAGUES

1. Water turned to blood
2. Frogs
3. Gnats
4. Flies
5. Death of animals
6. Boils
7. Hail
8. Locusts
9. Darkness for three days
10. Death of firstborn sons

Aaron stretched out his hands and all the water in Egypt turned to blood. There was blood in the streams, blood in the wells, and blood in the jars inside people's homes. The Egyptians had nothing to drink. They couldn't bathe or wash their clothes. They couldn't water their crops or their animals. The air smelled like blood and dead fish.

Was Pharaoh amazed by God's great power? Did he worry about the suffering of his people? Did he let the Israelites go? No. Several verses in Exodus say Pharaoh's heart was very hard. The people of Egypt had to dig along the Nile to find fresh water.

We don't know how long the water in Egypt was turned to blood or how the blood finally went away. But one week later, Pharaoh refused to let the Israelites go (see *Frogs in the Bed and* *Flies in the Soup* on p. 8). It took ten signs before Pharaoh listened to God and let the Israelites go.

Walls of Water

Exodus 14:21–31; Joshua 3

What makes water water? Each tiny part, or molecule, is made of two hydrogen atoms and one oxygen atom. When water is in liquid form, it flows and takes the shape of its container. If you put water in a round glass, it will be round. If you pour it into a square mug, it will be square. But it won't just stand up on its own.

After God sent ten plagues, Pharaoh finally let the Israelites go. Moses led the freed people into the wilderness. They camped by the shore of the Red Sea. The Israelites were already worried about where to go when things got worse. Pharaoh changed his mind and chased after them with his entire army. It looked like the Israelites were trapped.

God told Moses to stretch out his hand over the water. A strong wind blew the water back on either side. The Israelites were able to walk right across the dry seabed with a wall of water on either side. All night long, the wind held the water back, and the Israelites escaped. When the Egyptians followed them, the walls of water came crashing down. All the Egyptians were killed.

As soon as the priests' feet touched the water's edge, dry ground appeared. The Jordan River piled up in a great heap upstream.

The book of Joshua describes a similar story. Joshua was leading the Israelites to the land of Canaan. First, they had to cross the Jordan River during its flood season. Thousands of people, with all their animals and possessions, would have to cross the river that was flowing over its banks.

Joshua sent the priests ahead first, and they carried the ark of the covenant. As soon as their feet touched the water's edge, dry ground appeared. The Jordan River stopped flowing. The water piled up in a great heap upstream.

The priests waited while all the Israelites crossed on dry ground. When all the people had crossed the river, the priests followed. As soon as the priests stepped out of the riverbed, the Jordan flowed again.

did You KNOW?

- About 65% of your body is made of water.
- Water covers about three-fourths of the earth's surface.
- The chemical formula for water is H_2O.
- H_2O can be liquid (water), solid (ice), or gas (vapor).

A Strange Source of Water

Exodus 17:1–7; Numbers 20:2–13

People can survive about three weeks without food but only three days without water. When God led the Israelites to a place with no water, they became worried. "Give us water," they said to Moses. The people quarreled with Moses and complained that he had brought them into the wilderness to die of thirst.

Moses could not create water, so he prayed. God told Moses to take his staff and go to the rock at Horeb. "I will stand before you," God said. "You shall strike the rock, and water shall come out of it" (Exodus 17:6).

Moses obeyed God. The elders of the people saw him strike the rock with his staff. Clean, fresh water came pouring out. Finally, the people and their animals could drink.

God told Moses to strike a rock with his staff and water would come out of it. It did!

90

(Nearly) Dying of Thirst

Most people can only live a few days without water, but a man from Austria went much longer without water. In 1979, police forgot about eighteen-year-old Andreas Mihavecz in a prison cell. The young man survived eighteen days without food or water!

The Israelites faced the same problem again later, and again they complained to Moses: "There is no water to drink" (Numbers 20:5).

Moses and Aaron fell facedown before God. This time, God's instructions were a little different. God told Moses to take his staff, gather the people, and "tell the rock" to give them water (Numbers 20:8).

Moses took his staff (check). He gathered all the people (check). But he did not speak to the rock. Instead, he struck it two times with his staff. The rock poured out fresh water, and the people had plenty to drink. But God punished Moses and Aaron for disobeying him—Moses had struck the rock instead of speaking to the rock. Because Moses and Aaron had not obeyed God, he did not allow them to enter the land of Canaan with the Israelites.

did you KNOW?

Moses and Aaron weren't the only Israelites who didn't get to enter the land of Canaan. After the Israelites left Egypt, they grumbled, complained, and disobeyed God. For that reason, God kept them in the wilderness for forty years. All the Israelites who were twenty years or older when they left Egypt died during those forty years— except for Joshua and Caleb, two men who obeyed God and were allowed to enter the land of Canaan (Numbers 32:11–13).

Parting the Jordan (Twice)

2 Kings 2:7–15

The Olympic Games begin with the lighting of a fire. First, the flame travels from Olympia, Greece, to the site of the games. Runners carry torches and pass the flame from one torch to the next until the flame reaches its destination. The saying "pass the torch" may have come from this tradition. It means that one person ends their role and gives the responsibilities to the next person.

Before the prophet Elijah "passed the torch" to Elisha, he performed one last miracle on the water of the Jordan River. After Elijah went up to heaven, Elisha performed his first miracle—also on the water of the Jordan.

Elisha followed his teacher toward the Jordan River. Even though Elijah asked him to stay behind, Elisha would not leave him. Off in the distance, fifty prophets watched the two men. Elijah took off his cloak and rolled it up. He struck the water of the Jordan. The water parted, leaving dry ground in front of them.

After the two men crossed the river, Elijah was taken up to heaven in a whirlwind. Now, it was time for Elisha to perform his first miracle. With fifty prophets looking on, Elisha took up Elijah's cloak and struck the Jordan River. "Where is the LORD, the God of Elijah?" he asked.

Once again, the water parted and Elisha walked to the other side of the river. "The spirit of Elijah rests on Elisha," the prophets said. Elijah had passed the torch to his student, Elisha.

Quick Quiz

1. Who else crossed the parted water of the Jordan River?
2. What other miracles did Elisha repeat after Elijah?

Elijah was taken up to heaven in a whirlwind.

Answers:
1. Joshua and all the Israelites and their animals (see *Walls of Water* on p. 88)
2. Bringing someone back to life and making food last longer (see *Great Teacher, God's Power* on p. 80)

You Can "Dew" It!

Judges 6:11–16, 33–40

Gideon was not the person most likely to be chosen to lead an army. He was the least important member of his family. His clan was the weakest in his tribe. His tribe was one of the smallest in Israel. His enemy was the mighty Midianites. Not even Gideon thought he could save Israel.

But God chose him to defeat Israel's enemy. God said to Gideon, "I will be with you," and he promised that Gideon would defeat the Midianites.

The Midianites joined with Israel's other enemies. They crossed the Jordan River and camped nearby. It was time for Gideon to act. He blew a trumpet and sent out messengers to gather his army. Israel's soldiers came to his side.

Gideon was the least important member of his family, and his clan was the weakest in his tribe.

A Man Who Obeyed at Night

Before Gideon called his army, God told Gideon to take down his father's altar to the god Baal. In its place, Gideon was to build an altar to God and sacrifice a bull. Gideon obeyed, but he did it at night so the people of the town wouldn't see. In the morning, they found out it was Gideon who had destroyed their altar. They were angry and wanted to kill Gideon! Gideon's father told the people that if Baal were a real god, he could fight for himself.

did you KNOW?

Dew comes from water vapor in the air. Grass, cars, swing sets, and other objects cool off during the night. The air that touches these cool objects can't hold on to its water vapor, so little drops of water form. This is called condensation. It also happens on the outside of your glass if you have a cold drink on a hot day.

Gideon wanted a sign from God that the Israelites would defeat the Midianites. He put a wool fleece on the ground. He asked God to make the fleece wet with dew and the ground around it dry. In the morning, Gideon found that the ground was dry. The fleece was so wet with dew that he squeezed out enough water to fill a bowl.

That was a good sign, but Gideon wanted one more. He put the fleece on the ground again. This time he asked God make the fleece dry while the ground around it was wet with dew. In the morning, God had done so. Now Gideon was sure that God would keep his promise.

Gideon and his men went on to defeat the Midianite army (see *Less Is More* on p. 44), just as God had promised.

God's Great Promise

Genesis 15

Some people might picture God as a man with a flowing white beard or as a spirit floating in the clouds. The Bible gives us many different descriptions of God. When God came to Abram in a vision, he said, "I am your shield; your reward shall be very great" (Genesis 15:1).

Abram was confused and wondered what God meant by the vision. Abram had no children, so when he died, his servant would inherit the things he left behind.

In the vision, God made an important promise to Abram: "Your very own son will be your heir." God also said, "Look toward heaven, and number the stars." Then God told Abram that he would have as many offspring as there are stars.

The Bible gives us many descriptions of God. He told Abram he would be his shield.

God Speaks to Abram

This vision wasn't the first time or the last time God spoke to Abram. Before this, God told him to go to Canaan (Genesis 12). It was the land God promised him. Later, God appeared to Abram and told him that his wife would have a son (Genesis 18). God spoke to Abram other times as well.

Abram believed God's promise. He sacrificed a cow, a goat, a ram, a turtledove, and a pigeon. Then Abram fell into a deep sleep. A great darkness came over him, and God told him what would happen to his offspring. They would have some hard times. They would even become slaves. But someday they would return to their own land.

When the sun went down, a smoking pot and a blazing torch passed through Abram's sacrifice. God promised the land to Abram's offspring.

God kept his promise. God changed Abram's name to Abraham. Abraham became the father of Isaac, who became the father of Jacob. Jacob's name changed to Israel, and he became the father of the Israelites.

FAMILY TREE

King David

Twelve tribes of Israel

Jacob

Isaac

Abraham

Dreaming on a Stone Pillow

Genesis 28:10–22

"This bed is as hard as a rock!" That's what Jacob might have thought as he lay down one night. He was traveling far to find a wife. He had to sleep on the hard ground and used a stone for a pillow. But he had an amazing dream.

In the dream, he saw a ladder stretching from earth to heaven. Angels climbed up and down the ladder. At the top stood God. He made many promises to Jacob:

God sometimes communicated through dreams. In this one he stood at the top of a ladder.

"I am the LORD, *the God of Abraham your father and the God of Isaac. The land on which you lie I will give to you and to your offspring. Your offspring shall be like the dust of the earth, and you shall spread abroad to the west and to the east and to the north and to the south, and in you and your offspring shall all the families of the earth be blessed. Behold, I am with you and will keep you wherever you go, and will bring you back to this land. For I will not leave you until I have done what I have promised you."*
(Genesis 28:13–15)

Jacob woke up amazed. He thought God must be there with him! He poured oil over his stone pillow. He made a promise: "If God will be with me . . . then the LORD shall be my God" (Genesis 18:20–21).

98

Jacob's Ladder

This event from the Bible inspired the name for many objects. "Jacob's Ladder" is the name of a type of plant. It's also an old-fashioned toy made of wood and ribbons. It's even a machine people use to work out in a gym!

did YOU KNOW?

Everyone dreams every night, but we don't remember all our dreams. You start a new dream about every ninety minutes. The first dream of the night is about five minutes long, and they get longer as the night goes on. When you dream, your eyes move around quickly even though your eyelids are closed!

Dreams Come True

Genesis 37

Can you imagine what it would be like to have ten older brothers who all hate you? That's what happened to Joseph, and his dreams only made matters worse.

Joseph's brothers were already frustrated with him before he told them his dreams. First of all, their father favored Joseph. Then, their father gave Joseph a special colorful robe. This made the brothers very jealous.

One day, Joseph told his brothers about a dream he had. In Joseph's dream, he and his brothers were out in the field cutting grain. Joseph's bunch of grain got up and stood tall, while his brothers' bunches of grain all bowed down around it. The brothers did not like Joseph's dream. Was Joseph telling them he wanted to rule over them? Now they hated him even more.

Joseph telling his dreams made his brothers so angry they sold him into slavery.

JOSEPH'S BROTHERS

- Reuben
- Simeon
- Levi
- Judah
- Dan
- Naphtali
- Gad
- Asher
- Issachar
- Zebulun
- Benjamin

Then Joseph had another dream. He told his brothers and his father, "The sun, the moon, and eleven stars were bowing down to me" (Genesis 37:9). Did Joseph think that his brothers and even his father and mother would bow down to him?

These dreams made Joseph's brothers so angry and jealous they planned to kill him. They kidnapped Joseph and threw him in a pit. Instead of killing him, they sold him into slavery. They made their father think Joseph was killed by a wild animal.

According to the story, years later Joseph's dreams came true. He became an important ruler in Egypt. During a famine, his hungry brothers came looking for food. They did not recognize Joseph. They bowed down to him. What did Joseph do? He forgave his brothers and provided care for them and their families during the famine. Joseph told his brothers, "You meant evil against me, but God meant it for good" (Genesis 50:20).

Check It Out!

The story of Joseph was made into a musical called *Joseph and the Amazing Technicolor Dreamcoat*. You can enjoy the song about his dreams called "Joseph's Dreams." Search online to find many versions of this performance, including some by young students. (The song mentions eleven brothers, but Joseph's younger brother, Benjamin, was probably too young to take part in his kidnapping.)

What Does It Mean?

Genesis 40

Joseph had meaningful dreams, but Genesis says God gave him the ability to understand other people's dreams too.

Many years passed between the time Joseph's brothers sold him into slavery until the time he became an important ruler in Egypt. During those years,

Joseph spent time in jail, even though he did nothing wrong.

Joseph spent time in jail, even though he did nothing wrong. One day, two new prisoners joined him. One was a cupbearer and one was a baker. They had served Pharaoh until he became angry with them and had them arrested.

One morning, both men reported that they'd had strange dreams. They told their dreams to Joseph, and God helped him understand their meanings.

In the cupbearer's dream, a vine with three branches grew grapes. The cupbearer squeezed the grapes in Pharaoh's cup and gave it to him to drink.

Joseph told him what the dream meant. In three days, Pharaoh would return the cupbearer to his job. Joseph had one request for the cupbearer: "Remember me, and please mention me to Pharaoh, and so get me out of this house" (Genesis 40:14).

Next, the baker told Joseph his dream. "I also had a dream: there were three cake baskets on my head, and in the uppermost basket there were all sorts of baked food for Pharaoh, but the birds were eating it out of the basket on my head" (Genesis 40:16–17).

Joseph did not have good news for the baker. In three days, he explained, Pharaoh would have the baker killed.

Three days later, Pharaoh had a big birthday party. He called for his cupbearer and baker from jail. He gave the cupbearer his job back, but he had the baker killed. It all happened just as Joseph said.

Did the cupbearer remember Joseph? Did he ask Pharaoh to let Joseph out of jail? No, he forgot about

Why Was Joseph in Jail?

As a slave, Joseph worked hard for an important man named Potiphar. Soon, Potiphar put Joseph in charge of his entire house. God made Joseph successful in all he did. Potiphar trusted Joseph and took good care of him. One day, Potiphar's wife told lies about Joseph. Potiphar believed the lies and put Joseph in jail. But even in jail, God was with Joseph. Soon, Joseph was in charge of the whole jail.

him. Joseph waited in jail for two more years. Finally, Pharaoh had his own strange dreams, and then the cupbearer remembered Joseph (see *From Prisoner to Ruler* on p. 104).

From Prisoner to Ruler

Genesis 41

Pharaoh was upset. He'd had two strange dreams, and he didn't know what they meant. He called for his magicians and wise men. No one understood Pharaoh's dreams.

The royal cupbearer spoke up, telling about when he and the baker were in jail and both of them had dreams. The cupbearer described a young Hebrew man named Joseph who told them the meanings of their dreams. The cupbearer told Pharaoh that Joseph's explanations of their dreams came true.

Right away, Pharaoh called for Joseph. He asked if Joseph could understand his dreams. Joseph explained that he could not understand the dreams, but that God could.

"In my dream I was standing on the banks of the Nile," Pharaoh said. "Seven cows, plump and attractive, came up out of the Nile and fed in the reed grass. Seven other cows came up after them, poor and very ugly and thin. . . . And the thin, ugly cows ate up the first seven plump cows" (Genesis 41:17–20).

Then Pharaoh told Joseph his second dream: Seven full, healthy ears of grain grew on one stalk. Seven withered, unhealthy ears grew after the good ones. The unhealthy ears swallowed the good ones.

Pharaoh's dreams showed he needed to put a wise man in charge.

God showed Joseph how to explain Pharaoh's dreams. Joseph told Pharaoh that soon Egypt would have seven good years with plenty of food. But then there would be seven years of awful famine when there would not be any food.

This was bad news. Joseph told Pharaoh to put a wise man in charge of the land of Egypt who would store up food for the people during the good years. This way, the people wouldn't starve during the bad years.

Pharaoh thought this was a good idea. Whom should he choose? Pharaoh wanted someone who had the "Spirit of God" in him. Pharaoh chose Joseph. Joseph worked hard to gather

and store food during the seven years before the famine. Many people were saved because Joseph listened to God and explained Pharaoh's dreams.

A New Job

Joseph quickly went from being a slave in jail to being in charge of all Egypt. He ruled the palace and all the land. Pharaoh commanded all the Egyptians to obey his orders and bow down to him. Only Pharaoh had more power than Joseph. With his new job, Joseph was given Pharaoh's ring, fine clothes, and a gold chain. His name was changed to Zaphenath-paneah, and he was given an Egyptian wife. He rode in a chariot through the land.

Speaking for God

Isaiah 6:1–8

In the Bible, the story of Isaiah the prophet begins with Isaiah's description of his amazing vision of God:

I saw the Lord sitting upon a throne, high and lifted up; and the train of his robe filled the temple. Above him stood the seraphim. Each had six wings: with two he covered his face, and with two he covered his feet, and with two he flew. And one called to another and said:

"Holy, holy, holy is the Lord of hosts; the whole earth is full of his glory!"

And the foundations of the thresholds shook at the voice of him who called, and the house was filled with smoke. (Isaiah 6:1–4).

What did Isaiah think of this amazing vision? He did not feel worthy to see God. "I am a man of unclean lips," he cried.

One of the seraphim took a burning coal from the altar. He flew to Isaiah and touched the coal to Isaiah's mouth. It took away Isaiah's sin. Now he was ready to serve God.

Isaiah served as God's messenger for many years. He warned Israel to turn from sin. He told the people about God's salvation. He brought messages of healing (see *Back from the Brink of Death* on p. 38). These messages are found in the book of Isaiah.

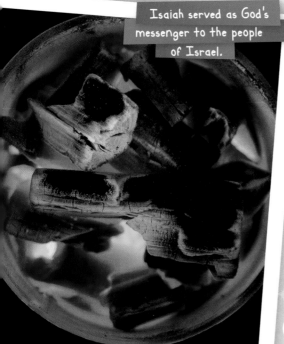

Isaiah served as God's messenger to the people of Israel.

Seven Hundred Years Later

The Israelites remembered the words of Isaiah for hundreds of years. Long after the prophet died, other writers quoted him. Some of Isaiah's words ended up in the New Testament:

- "The voice of one crying in the wilderness: 'Prepare the way of the Lord, make his paths straight' " (Mark 1:3; Isaiah 40:3).

- "Behold, the virgin shall conceive and bear a son, and they shall call his name Immanuel" (Matthew 1:23; Isaiah 7:14).

- "Like a sheep he was led to the slaughter and like a lamb before its shearer is silent, so he opens not his mouth" (Acts 8:32; Isaiah 53:7).

- "By his wounds you have been healed" (1 Peter 2:24; Isaiah 53:5).

FAST FACTS

Things you may not know about the **Hebrew Bible**:

- **Longest book** by number of verses: Psalms

- **Shortest book** by number of verses: Obadiah

- **Longest word:** Maher-shalal-hash-baz (Isaiah 8:1)

- **Shortest verse** in the Bible: "He said." (Job 3:2, NIV)

- **Longest verse** in the Bible: Esther 8:9

The King's Mystery

Daniel 2

Sometimes we have crazy dreams, and we want to know if they mean something. It's hard to know the meaning of a dream—especially if we can't remember the dream.

King Nebuchadnezzar had a troubling dream. He made an impossible challenge for his wise men. He commanded them to tell him the meaning of his dream, but he wouldn't tell anyone what his dream was about! The king threatened to have the wise men killed if they could not tell him the meaning.

Of course, the wise men did not know the king's dream and could not tell him its meaning. King Nebuchadnezzar sent out officials to kill all the wise men in the kingdom.

Daniel and his friends prayed to God. They asked God to show them the meaning of the king's dream so they wouldn't be killed.

God answered their prayer. That night, Daniel had a vision. It showed him the meaning of the king's dream. Daniel praised God, saying, "He gives wisdom to the wise" (Daniel 2:21).

King Nebuchadnezzar commanded his wise men to tell him what he had dreamed!

did you KNOW?

Daniel and his friends were Israelites taken from their homeland to Babylon as exiles. They were strong, smart, and handsome, so they were chosen to get special training to serve the king. Nebuchadnezzar found that they were ten times wiser than anyone else in the kingdom.

Daniel went before the king and said, "No wise men, enchanters, magicians, or astrologers can show to the king the mystery that the king has asked, but there is a God in heaven who reveals mysteries" (Daniel 2:27–28).

King Nebuchadnezzar listened as Daniel described his whole dream. The king had seen a huge statue in the dream. It had a gold head, silver arms and chest, and a bronze belly and thighs. Its legs and feet were made of iron and clay. A rock smashed the statue into pieces. The pieces were all swept away by the wind, but the rock became a huge mountain.

Then Daniel explained the dream. The statue stood for different kingdoms that would rise and fall. The rock that smashed them stood for God's kingdom. It would crush the other kingdoms and last forever.

The king was amazed. He fell at Daniel's feet and said, "Truly, your God is God of gods and Lord of kings, and a revealer of mysteries" (Daniel 2:47). He gave Daniel many gifts and made him a ruler over Babylon. Even Daniel's friends Shadrach, Meshach, and Abednego were given important jobs.

Nebuchadnezzar, however, did not choose to worship God. Soon, he had Shadrach, Meshach, and Abednego thrown into a furnace because they wouldn't worship his statue (see *Is It Warm in Here?* on p. 72). Then, he ignored Daniel's warnings to honor God (see *From Palace to Pasture* on p. 60).

A Vision of the Future

Daniel 7

What has iron teeth, bronze claws, and ten horns on its head? That's what Daniel wanted to know! He saw this terrifying beast in a dream.

In Daniel's vision, four beasts came up out of a great sea. One looked like a lion with eagle's wings, another looked like a bear, and another was like a four-headed leopard. The most frightening was the fourth beast. It had ten horns

This vision was troubling to Daniel. A heavenly worshiper explained it.

and used its iron teeth to eat up victims. Daniel watched as the beast was killed and thrown into a fire.

Daniel saw someone called "the Ancient of Days." He had white hair and white clothes and sat on a throne that blazed with fire. Daniel also saw a "son of man" appear in the clouds. Everyone worshiped the son of man, and he was given a kingdom that will last forever.

This vision was troubling to Daniel. What did it all mean? A heavenly worshiper explained it. The beasts stood for earthly kings and their kingdoms. The fourth beast, and fourth kingdom, was the strongest. Its ten horns stood for ten kings. But in the end, God's kingdom will last forever. Everyone will worship and obey him.

Two years later, Daniel saw another vision (see *Daniel's Helper* on p. 76). Even though God helped him understand the visions, Daniel was still puzzled. People who study the Bible today still wonder about these visions.

Look Again

Does this vision sound familiar? Compare it to King Nebuchadnezzar's dream (see *The King's Mystery* on p. 108).

Daniel's Vision	King Nebuchadnezzar's Dream
Four beasts	Statue made of four parts
Beasts stand for kingdoms	Statue stands for kingdoms
Beast is killed	Statue is destroyed
God's kingdom lasts forever	God's kingdom lasts forever

did you KNOW?

In the Bible, people are often upset by dreams and visions. Nebuchadnezzar was so troubled and afraid by his dreams that he couldn't sleep. After his visions, Daniel's face became pale and he was exhausted for days.

That's a Lot of Birthday Candles

Genesis 5:3–27

Jeanne Louise Calment of France was 122½ years old when she died in 1997. She holds the Guinness World Record for being the oldest person who ever lived. But according to the Bible, Jeanne isn't even in the top ten.

Many of the Bible characters in the book of Genesis lived very long lives—some into their 800s and 900s. Adam, the first man, lived to be 930 years old. Methuselah, Noah's grandfather, lived to be an amazing 969 years old! That's a lot longer than today's life span of about 78 years.

Bible characters in the book of Genesis lived into their 800s and 900s.

OLDEST PEOPLE IN THE BIBLE

1. Methuselah – 969 years old
2. Jared – 962 years old
3. Noah – 950 years old
4. Adam – 930 years old
5. Seth – 912 years old

A Tree Named Methuselah

Scientists say one of the oldest living things on Earth is a tree. It grows in the Inyo National Forest in California. This ancient Bristlecone Pine has been growing for over 4,700 years. Its name is Methuselah. The tree's exact location is kept secret so it can keep growing without being harmed.

The Bible doesn't tell us why these people lived so long. But according to the Bible's records of life spans, people began living shorter lives after the Flood. Noah's son Shem "only" lived to be 600 years old. Shem's son lived to be 438 years old. When Abram came along (about eight generations later), he only lived to be 175 years old. Moses lived just 120 years. By the time the book of Psalms was written, it

seems people were living about as long as they do today. "The years of our life are seventy, or even . . . eighty" (Psalm 90:10).

It seems Methuselah will always hold the record for most candles on his birthday cake.

Un-Identical Twins

Genesis 25:24–26, 27:1–29

Do you know any identical twins? It can be surprising to meet two people who look almost exactly alike. But not all twins are identical. Some have different eye, hair, and skin color. Jacob and Esau from the Bible were not identical. They didn't look alike.

Isaac and Rebekah had waited a long time for children. Isaac prayed to God, asking for children. When Rebekah became pregnant, she was carrying twins!

Jacob's mother guided him to deceive his father, Isaac.

Twins in the Bible

Jacob and Esau are the first twins recorded in the Bible. Later, Jacob's son Judah has twin sons named Perez and Zerah (Genesis 38:27–30).

LONG-LOST BROTHER

Jacob's trick made Esau very mad. Jacob ran away and didn't see his brother for years. Finally, he returned to his brother, and Esau forgave him (see *A Wrestling Injury* on p. 50).

The time came for the babies to be born. Esau was born first. His body was red and very hairy, "like a hairy cloak" (Genesis 25:25). Jacob was born second, grabbing his brother's heel.

Years later, Jacob's mother guided him to deceive his father, Isaac, who was old and blind. Rebekah instructed Jacob to dress up as his twin and trick Isaac into blessing him instead of Esau. But what if Isaac reached out and felt Jacob's smooth skin? Jacob's mother disguised him by wrapping goatskins around his arms and neck. The disguise worked! Isaac felt the thick hair and thought he was touching his son Esau. Esau must have been hairy, indeed.

The Strongest Man

Judges 16

Each year, men from around the world compete for the title of World's Strongest Man. They carry refrigerators, drag heavy anchors, and pull huge trucks. The competitors train for years to build their muscles. They lift weights and follow a special diet.

The strongest man in the Bible, however, followed a different set of rules: no wine, no unclean food, no haircuts. Samson was a Nazirite, which means he was set apart for God to lead Israel. His strength didn't come from lifting weights but from the "Spirit of the LORD" (Judges 14:6, 19, 15:14).

During Samson's life, he tore apart a lion with his bare hands. He struck down his enemies, once killing a thousand men with nothing but the jawbone of a donkey. Samson even tore down the doors of a city gate and carried them to the top of a hill. (To read more about Samson, see *A Strange Container for Honey* on p. 22 and *Samson's Revenge* on p. 52.)

The strongest man in the Bible followed these rules: no wine, no unclean food, no haircuts.

As strong as he was, Samson was no match for Delilah's constant pressure and urging. He had fallen in love with Delilah, but she had plans to betray him. She questioned Samson every day, trying to learn the secret of his strength.

Finally, Samson gave in. He told her, "If my head is shaved, then my strength will leave me" (Judges 16:17). Right away, Delilah told this to Samson's enemies. They cut his hair and poked out his eyes. Samson had no strength to fight back. He was taken to prison.

Slowly, Samson's hair began to grow back. One day, his enemies brought him to the crowded temple. They wanted to laugh at the weak, blind Samson. "O Lord GOD," Samson prayed. "Please remember me and please strengthen me only this once" (Judges 16:28). Samson reached out and put his hands on the pillars of the temple. With a mighty push, he knocked the building down. The world's strongest man died along with many of his enemies.

did you KNOW?

Samson's birth was announced by an angel. He told Samson's mother that she would have a son. He said this son would be a Nazirite who would save Israel from the Philistines. The angel appeared again to Samson's father. When Samson's parents offered a sacrifice to God during the angel's visit, the angel rose toward heaven in the flame and disappeared.

The Wisest Man

1 Kings 3

If you could have one wish—any wish—what would it be? King Solomon had this chance, and he didn't waste it. When God came to him in a dream and offered him anything he asked for, Solomon chose wisdom.

Solomon was young and unsure of how to rule his people. He wanted the wisdom to know right from wrong. God was happy with Solomon's request and gave Solomon wisdom. God told Solomon that he would be wiser than anyone who has ever lived.

Solomon once offered to cut a baby in half so two women could share him. Why?

Solomon's Great Wealth

Solomon could have wished for anything, and he chose wisdom. As a reward, God also gave him honor and great wealth. Solomon owned 1,400 chariots, 40,000 stalls for horses, and 12,000 horsemen. He sat on a throne of ivory and gold. Other nations paid him in gold, spices, food, and other goods. Solomon was richer than any other king on earth.

A book of Wisdom

According to the Bible, people came from all over the world to hear Solomon's words of wisdom. You can find everyday wisdom in the Bible in the book of Proverbs. For example, "Hatred stirs up strife, but love covers all offenses" (10:12).

The Israelites came to Solomon with their problems. One day, two women came to Solomon for help. They were fighting over a baby.

The first woman explained that the two women lived in the same house and each had a baby boy. "This woman's son died in the night" she said (1 Kings 3:19). She told Solomon that while she slept, the other woman swapped her dead son for the son who was alive. She said, "But when I looked at him closely in the morning, behold, he was not the child that I had borne" (1 Kings 3:21).

The second woman said, "No, the living child is mine and the dead child is yours" (1 Kings 3:22).

The two women argued and argued. What could Solomon do? There was no such thing as a DNA test in those days. Instead, he did something very wise.

"Bring me a sword," Solomon commanded. "Divide the living child in two, and give half to the one and half to the other" (1 Kings 3:24–25). This might sound like a crazy solution, but it was very wise. The real mother would not want her baby to be harmed.

One of the women called out to Solomon, "Give her the living child, and by no means put him to death" (1 Kings 3:26).

This must be the true mother, Solomon realized. Everyone was amazed by the king's great wisdom.

The Great Flood

Genesis 7

The people of Meghalaya, India, live much of their lives under big reed umbrellas called knups. That's because Meghalaya is the wettest place on earth. It receives 467 inches of rain per year, which is extreme but not unnatural. The nearby bay and high plateau make Meghalaya a natural home for heavy rain.

The first rain recorded in the book of Genesis was during Noah's life. According to the Bible, God had seen wickedness all over the earth and decided to destroy his creation. Genesis 6:9 describes Noah as "a righteous man" who "walked with God." Only he and his family would be saved from God's great flood.

The first rain recorded in the book of Genesis was after Noah got on the ark.

FAST FACTS

Tallest land animal: **giraffe**

Heaviest land animal:
African elephant

Fastest land animal: **cheetah**

Fastest bird:
peregrine falcon

Longest-living land animal:
Galapagos giant tortoise

Genesis 7:11–12 explains that once Noah's family and the animals were on the ark, "all the fountains of the great deep burst forth, and the windows of the heavens were opened. And rain fell upon the earth forty days and forty nights."

Floodwaters filled the earth and covered mountain peaks. All living things, except those inside the ark and animals that could survive in water, died. For 150 days, water covered the earth.

Finally, God sent a wind and the waters began to go down. It took months for dry land to appear again. It took even longer for people and animals to fill the earth once again. God made a promise to never again destroy the whole earth with a flood (see *A Sign in the Skies* on p. 64).

Escape from Sodom

Genesis 19:12–29

History is filled with reports of strange rains. Red, white, black, and yellow raindrops have fallen to earth. Fish, frogs, and golf balls have rained from the sky. Scientists often blame these strange rains on tornados and waterspouts.

The book of Genesis tells us that God once sent a rain that was not only strange but also very dangerous. Two angels visited the wicked city of Sodom. There, they stayed with a good man named Lot. The sinful men of the city tried to break down Lot's door.

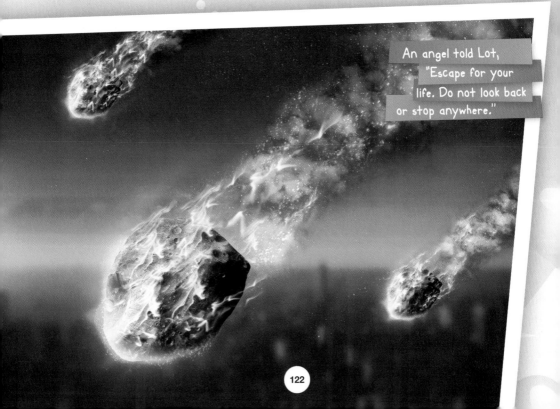

An angel told Lot, "Escape for your life. Do not look back or stop anywhere."

Sodom's Last Chance

God visited Abraham and revealed his plan to destroy the cities of Sodom and Gomorrah because they were so full of wickedness. Abraham pleaded with God. He asked if God would refrain from destroying a city if there were fifty good people living there. Or just forty. Or even just thirty, twenty, or ten. God sent his angels to look for ten good people in Sodom, but they could not find even ten.

One of the angels told Lot, "Escape for your life. Do not look back or stop anywhere in the valley" (Genesis 19:17).

Lot escaped with his wife and two daughters. The two young men who were engaged to Lot's daughters thought Lot was joking and did not escape with them. Sadly, Lot's wife did not make it out alive (see *A Strange Way to Go* on p. 136).

At sunrise, God sent a strange and terrible rain. Burning sulfur fell from the sky on the wicked cities. It killed the people and destroyed the buildings. It ruined all the fields where they grew food. Even from far away, Abraham

did you KNOW?

There are 118 known elements, and these are included on the periodic table. The abbreviation for sulfur is the letter S. Here are some other facts you might find interesting about sulfur:

- Sulfur is a yellowish substance that can be found near volcanoes, geysers, and hot springs.
- Plants and animals both need sulfur to survive. Even humans have sulfur in our bodies.
- Hydrogen sulfide (a gas formed from sulfur and hydrogen) smells like rotten eggs. This gas is often found in underground water, which is why some water from wells smells horrible!
- Sulfur by itself is nontoxic, but if it is part of an acid, it's very toxic.
- One of Jupiter's moons is yellowish in color because of the presence of sulfur.

(Lots's uncle) could see thick, dark smoke rising from the cities.

Was this a meteor shower? Or a volcanic eruption? Whatever destroyed these cities, Genesis 19 says it was sent by God as punishment.

Strange Skies

Exodus 9:22–26, 10:21–23

Rain can ruin your baseball game. Snow can close down roads. But hail can actually kill. Huge chunks of ice falling through the air can cause major damage. That's what happened when God sent the worst storm the Egyptians had ever seen.

Pharaoh would not let the Israelites go. God had turned the Nile to blood (see *No Swimming* on p. 86). He'd sent plagues of frogs, flies, and gnats (see *Frogs in the Bed and Flies in the Soup* on p. 8). Still, Pharaoh did not budge.

Moses warned Pharaoh that God would send terrible hail. Some Egyptians listened and brought their slaves and animals in from the fields. Others did not listen. The clouds grew thick. Thunder boomed and lightning flashed. Hail crashed down.

Hail destroyed the crops growing in the fields. It ripped branches off trees. It even killed people and animals who were left outside. The only safe place was Goshen, where the Israelites lived. No hail fell on the Israelites.

Did Pharaoh obey God after the hail? No. He promised to let the Israelites go, but he didn't keep his promise. God sent a plague of locusts. Still Pharaoh did not let the people go. Next, darkness fell upon the land.

Hail crashed down when God sent the worst storm the Egyptians had ever seen.

For three days, no light shone in Egypt. At night, there was no moon or stars. The daytime was just as dark. The Egyptians couldn't see anything or move about. Meanwhile, the Israelites still had light where they lived.

did YOU KNOW?

In Joshua 10, when Joshua led the Israelites in a battle against five kings, the sun stood still in the sky. For a whole day, the sun hung in the middle of the sky and the moon did not move. Joshua and his soldiers fought and won. God also sent hail to strike down the enemy army as they ran away.

Stand Back!

Exodus 19

"In [God's] hand are the depths of the earth; the heights of the mountains are his also" (Psalm 95:4). This Bible verse really comes to life in the story of the Israelites at Mount Sinai.

Moses led the people of Israel out of Egypt and into the wilderness. After two months, they stopped at Mount Sinai. God told Moses to get the people ready, because he was coming down onto the mountain.

Moses put limits around the foot of the mountain so the people wouldn't get too close. God had told him, "Whoever touches the mountain shall be put to death" (Exodus 19:12).

The Israelites spent three days getting ready. They washed their clothes. Then, they waited for God's trumpet blast.

When Moses spoke to God, "God answered him in thunder."

The Face of God

God told Moses, "You cannot see my face, for man shall not see me and live" (Exodus 33:20). To protect people, God set up rules about how close they could come to his presence. He told Moses to put borders around Mount Sinai. He had the priests separate a holy section of the tabernacle and later the temple. Several Bible passages record that people who stood in the presence of God or his angels were often terrified.

The morning began with thunder, lightning, and a thick cloud over the mountain. A loud trumpet blast made the people tremble. It was time to meet with God.

God came down on the mountain in fire. Smoke billowed up. An earthquake shook the whole mountain. The trumpet sound got louder and louder. When Moses spoke to God, "God answered him in thunder" (Exodus 19:19). Moses climbed to the top of the mountain to meet with God.

God spoke the Ten Commandments from the mountain (Exodus 20) (see *God's Top Ten* on p. 138).

did You KNOW?

Mount Sinai is also called Mount Horeb in the Bible. This is the same mountain where Moses saw the burning bush (see *The Burning Bush* on p. 66). It's where he struck the rock and water poured out (see *A Strange Source of Water* on p. 90). It's also where Elijah heard God's voice (see *God's Whisper* on p.130).

Dry Times

1 Kings 17:1, 7, 18:1–6, 41–46

By the Bible's standards, King Ahab was a bad, bad man. First Kings 16:30 and 21:25 says he did more evil than anyone ever had. He married a wicked woman. Together, they worshiped Baal. They had the prophets of God killed. King Ahab made God angrier than any king before him ever had.

God sent the prophet Elijah to speak to King Ahab. Elijah announced, "As the LORD, the God of Israel, lives, before whom I stand, there shall be neither dew nor rain these years, except by my word" (1 Kings 17:1).

This was bad news. How would the people survive a drought that would last years? They would have no water to drink. They wouldn't be able to give water to their animals. And what about their crops growing in the fields?

During the reign of evil King Ahab, no rain fell in Israel for over three years.

Drought Facts

A drought is a period of dry weather, when no or little rain or snow falls. It can last for a season or for many years. During a drought, soil can dry out, killing crops. Lakes, streams, and rivers can also dry up. The worst drought in United States history happened during the 1930s. During these "Dust Bowl" years, the south-central states suffered badly.

GOD'S SERVANT

Obadiah worked for King Ahab, but he loved and obeyed God. When Ahab and his wife began killing the prophets who served God, Obadiah took action. He took one hundred of God's prophets into the wilderness. There, he hid fifty in one cave and fifty in another cave. He snuck food and water to them to keep them alive.

In the story, no rain fell on the land for over three years. During this time, Elijah lived in the wilderness where birds brought him food (see *Ravens That Deliver Dinner* on p. 14). He also spent time living with a widow and her son (see *Your Son Is Alive!* on p. 78).

Finally, God told Elijah to face King Ahab once again. God commanded Elijah, "Go, show yourself to Ahab, and I will send rain upon the earth" (1 Kings 18:1).

Elijah returned to Samaria, where the people had very little food. He told Ahab to gather hundreds of false prophets for a showdown on Mount Carmel (see *One Against Many* on p. 48). Once Elijah had proven God's power, rain began to fall. The long drought was over.

God's Whisper

1 Kings 19:1–18

Your tone of voice is just as important as the words you speak. Suppose you tell a friend, "Sit down." If you use a soft, friendly tone, your friend will feel welcome.

In 1 Kings 19, the prophet Elijah heard God speak to him multiple times. Elijah was running for his life. He had just defeated the prophets of Baal, and Queen Jezebel wanted to kill him. Understandably, Elijah was afraid and discouraged. After traveling forty days and forty nights, he stopped to sleep in a cave on Mount Horeb.

God asked, "What are you doing here, Elijah?" (1 Kings 19:9).

Elijah explained that he had worked hard for God but now people were trying to kill him.

God told Elijah to go out of the cave and stand on the mountain.

In Exodus 19:19, God answered in thunder. This time he spoke gently, in a low whisper

Angels Helped Elijah

When Elijah ran from Jezebel, God sent an angel to help Elijah. "Arise and eat," the angel said (1 Kings 19:5). The angel gave Elijah fresh bread that was baked over hot stones and a jar of water. After food and rest, Elijah was able to travel for forty days and nights to meet God on Mount Horeb.

did you KNOW?

King Ahab and Queen Jezebel worshiped Baal and killed God's prophets. Finally, King Ahab was killed in battle. He was hit by an arrow and bled all day long until he died. Years later, Jezebel's servants pushed her out of a window. She fell to the ground and was run over by horses.

A powerful wind blew against the mountain. It was so strong it tore rocks apart. But God was not in the wind. Next, a strong earthquake shook the mountain. But God was not in the earthquake. After that came a roaring fire. But God was not in the fire. What would come next? Lightning? A volcanic eruption?

Finally, Elijah heard a low whisper. This was the gentle voice of God. Elijah put his cloak over his face and went to the mouth of the cave.

Again, God asked, "What are you doing here, Elijah?"(1 Kings 19:13).

Again, Elijah explained that people were trying to kill him.

God gave Elijah instructions to go back to work. Elijah would anoint two kings. He would also anoint the next prophet, Elisha. After hearing God's whisper, Elijah left his cave to serve God.

The Tower That Never Was

Genesis 11:1–9

¡Hola! Ni hao! Namaste! It can be fun to learn another language. But where did these different languages come from? According to the book of Genesis, it all started long ago, after the great flood.

The city was given the name *Babel* which sounds like the Hebrew word for "confused."

Noah's sons had children, and their children had children. Soon, there were many people on the earth once again. The people all spoke the same language. They could all understand one another. The people found a place to settle; then they got an idea.

The people had learned to make bricks. They could stack the bricks high and stick them together with mortar. They said, "Let us build ourselves a city and a tower with its top in the heavens" (Genesis 11:4).

God came down to see the city and said, "Behold, they are one people, and they have all one language, and this is only the beginning of what they will do" (Genesis 11:6).

God confused the people's language and dispersed the people all over the earth. They stopped building the city. It was given the name *Babel*, which sounds like the Hebrew word for "confused."

The people had to bid one another *ciao! Sayonara! Au revoir!*

Ancient Buildings

People long ago built different kinds of buildings. The pyramids in Egypt are burial tombs for kings. The Parthenon in Greece is a temple to a goddess. India's Great Stupa at Sanchi was built as a monument over the Buddha's ashes. Rome's Colosseum is an ancient theater. These buildings are all thousands of years old.

LEARN A LANGUAGE

Here's how to say "How are you?" in some different languages:

Spanish – *¿Cómo estás?*

Italian – *Come stai?*

Mandarin Chinese – *Nĭ hăo ma?*

Swahili – *Habari gani?*

French – *Comment allez-vous?*

Czech – *Jak se máš?*

Don't Call Her Grandma!

Genesis 17:15–22, 18:9–15, 21:2

Psalm 127:3 says, "Children are a gift from the LORD" (NLT). Most mothers give birth to their babies before the age of fifty. The record for the oldest mother to have a baby on her own is fifty-nine years old. When doctors help out, women as old as about seventy have had babies. Just imagine Sarah's surprise when God said she would have a baby at ninety years old!

Abraham and Sarah had no children of their own. They were very old. How would God keep his promise to make Abraham a great nation (see *God's Great Promise* on p. 96)?

When Sarah heard she would have a baby at ninety years old, she laughed, thinking it was impossible for her to have a child at her age.

134

did you KNOW?

Before the baby was born Sarah took matters into her own hands. Since it seemed they could not have children, she told Abraham to go start a family with her slave instead. Abraham had a son with Sarah's Egyptian slave, Hagar. They named the boy Ishmael. Later, after Isaac was born, Abraham sent Hagar and Ishmael away, but God took care of them.

God appeared to Abraham. God told him, "Sarah your wife shall bear you a son, and you shall call his name Isaac" (Genesis 17:19).

Abraham laughed. He was ninety-nine years old! But God promised that they would have a son in the next year.

Later God said to Abraham, "I will surely return to you about this time next year, and Sarah your wife shall have a son" (Genesis 18:10).

Sarah was listening to the conversation. When she heard this news, she laughed, thinking it was impossible for her to have a child at her age. But God said to Abraham, "Is anything too hard for the LORD?" (Genesis 18:14).

Just like God had promised, Abraham and Sarah had a baby boy.

FAST FACTS

Months when most babies are born: **August** and **September**

Average weight of a baby at birth: **7.5 pounds**

Average age of a first-time mother: **25 years old**

Number of babies born each day: **about 353,000**

They named their son Isaac, which means "he laughs." He made Abraham and Sarah very happy in their old age. (They probably looked more like grandparents or even great-grandparents than parents.)

A Strange Way to Go

Genesis 19:15–26

Many people died when God destroyed the cities of Sodom and Gomorrah (see *Escape from Sodom* on p. 122). But one of the strangest deaths happened outside the city that day.

Angels rescued Lot and his family before God destroyed Sodom. They entered Lot's house. They told the family to hurry and run for their lives!! They even took each person by the hand—Lot, his wife, and his two daughters—to lead them out of the city.

Before the destruction began, one of the angels gave one more command: "Do not look back or stop anywhere in the valley"(Genesis 19:17). They told the family to flee to the hills.

Lot didn't think they could make it as far as the hills. He asked that his family be allowed to escape to the small city of Zoar instead.

The Bible says Lot's wife looked back and became a pillar of salt.

Somewhere, either in the valley or in Zoar, Lot's wife died. We don't know exactly when or where it happened. We don't even know her name. The Bible only says, "But Lot's wife, behind him, looked back, and she became a pillar of salt" (Genesis 19:26).

What a strange event! Was the pillar tall and strong, like those on a building? Or was it the size and shape of Lot's wife? Did the salt look like fine, white table salt? Or something else? When did Lot and his daughters discover that she was gone?

The Bible doesn't tell us those answers. We don't even know how she could have turned into salt. All we know from the Bible is that Lot's wife did the opposite of what the angel told her to do. She looked back—and she suffered a fatal consequence.

did you KNOW?

Salt is a mineral made of sodium and chloride. It's the only rock that people eat. Every cell in your body contains salt, and it's possible to die from too little or too much salt in your body.

God's Top Ten

Exodus 31:18, 32:15–16, 19, 34:1–28

The Bible is a collection of words written by human authors. Within the pages of the Bible we find stories, histories, prophecies, laws, advice, and poems.

According to the book of Exodus, the only part of the Bible God wrote with his own hand was the Ten Commandments. On Mount Sinai, God spoke to Moses for a long time (see *Stand Back!* on p. 126). He told Moses how the Israelites should live and how to keep from sinning. Then God touched two tablets of stone. He used his finger to write out his laws. Exodus 32:16 says, "The tablets were the work of God, and the writing was the writing of God, engraved on the tablets."

The only part of the Bible God wrote with his own hand was the Ten Commandments.

The Ten Commandments

1. Do not have other gods besides the Lord your God.
2. Do not make an idol to worship.
3. Do not misuse the name of the Lord your God.
4. Keep the Sabbath day holy.
5. Honor your father and your mother.
6. Do not murder.
7. Keep your marriage promises.
8. Do not steal.
9. Do not lie.
10. Do not be jealous of other people's things.

What did Moses do with these special stone tablets? Well, he carried them down the mountain and then smashed them to pieces! That's right—Moses threw the tablets to the ground. He was angry because he saw people sinning. While he had been on the mountain talking to God, they built a golden calf to worship. As a punishment, about three thousand Israelites died that day.

"Cut for yourself two tablets of stone like the first," God commanded Moses. "And I will write on the tablets

MOSES TRIVIA

1. What does the name *Moses* mean? (Exodus 2:10)
2. What crime did Moses commit in Egypt? (Exodus 2:12)
3. What was Moses's job before God sent him to Pharaoh? (Exodus 3:1)
4. How old was Moses when he died? (Deuteronomy 34:7)

the words that were on the first tablets, which you broke" (Exodus 34:1). Again, God used his own finger to engrave his Ten Commandments on the tablets. This time, they were kept safely in the ark of the covenant.

Answers: 1. "draw out" 2. murder 3. shepherd 4. 120

Disappearing Acts

Genesis 5:24; Numbers 16

Isn't it frustrating to lose things? That permission slip you thought was in your backpack. The soccer cleat you need for the game in five minutes. These things didn't just disappear. The ground didn't just open up and swallow them. That kind of thing only seems to happen in the Bible.

We don't know much about Enoch, but the Bible tells us he "walked with God." It says he was the father of Methuselah and other sons and daughters. We can read that Enoch lived 365 years. But he didn't die after that. The Bible tells us "he was not, for God took him" (Genesis 5:24).

And that's it! Enoch didn't grow old and get sick and die. He wasn't killed. He just suddenly "was not." It was a very special disappearing act.

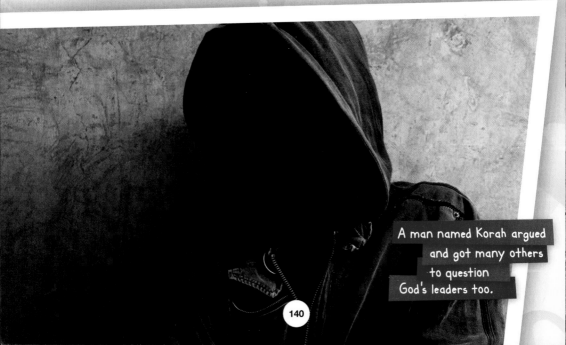

A man named Korah argued and got many others to question God's leaders too.

did you KNOW?

Enoch isn't the only person in the Bible who did not die. The prophet Elijah was taken up to heaven in a whirlwind.

In another story in the Bible, a man named Korah and some other men argued against Moses and Aaron. Korah accused Moses of acting like he was better than the rest of the people.

Moses told Korah and his followers to bring an offering to God. Moses told the people that if Korah and his followers died of natural causes, it would prove God didn't send Moses to lead them. Then Moses said, "If . . . the ground opens its mouth and swallows them," the people would "know that these men have despised the Lord" (Numbers 16:30).

As soon as Moses finished his warning, the ground split apart under their feet. "The earth opened its mouth and swallowed them up" (Numbers 16:32). Korah, his family, his followers, and all their possessions went down into the ground. "The earth closed over them" (Numbers 16:33), and they were gone.

It Gets Worse

Some of Korah's followers were making an offering to God when this happened. They did not get swallowed up with the others. Instead, God sent fire to kill these 250 wicked men.

Choosing Priests

Numbers 17

It was time to pick the man to lead the priests. Instead of leaving the decision up to Moses, God performed a sign to show that the choice was his.

Twelve leaders each gave their staff to Moses. One of them belonged to Aaron. Moses wrote the name of each leader on his staff.

Moses put the staffs in front of the ark of the covenant, where he met with God. Then God said, "The staff of the man whom I choose shall sprout" (Numbers 17:5). Moses left the staffs there overnight.

One man needed to lead the priests.

Fair Is Fair

How do you choose when you don't want to choose? Here are some ideas you can try:

- Flip a coin.
- Rock, paper, scissors.
- Draw straws (whoever chooses the short straw is "it").
- Pull names from a hat.
- Touch your nose (the last one to touch their nose is "it").

did you KNOW?

Of Jacob's twelve sons, Levi was third. Levi's descendants were not counted as a tribe like those of his brothers. Instead, the Levites became the priests and temple workers of Israel. Moses and Aaron were descended from Levi.

The next morning, Moses entered the tent to look at the staffs. One certainly looked different from the others. It hadn't just sprouted; it had also budded, blossomed, and grown almonds! God had made his choice clear.

And who do you think it was? The budding staff belonged to Aaron, Moses's brother. He and his sons were God's choice to become priests. God told Moses to keep Aaron's staff in front of the ark of the covenant. It would be a sign to the Israelites that he chose Aaron and they shouldn't grumble against God.

A Face Like the Sun

Exodus 34:27–35

TV commercials try to sell products that give you glowing skin. They tell you to use a certain soap or face cream. Moses did not use either, but his face glowed so brightly it got people's attention in a very good way.

Moses had been on Mount Sinai for forty days and forty nights. During that time, he did not eat or drink. Instead, he listened to God speak. God wrote the Ten Commandments on stone tablets (see *God's Top Ten* on p. 138). Finally, it was time for Moses to come down and lead the Israelites.

Moses's face was radiant. That means it gave off light.

Fasting in the Bible

Moses went forty days and nights without food or water—twice! Here are some others in the Hebrew Bible who fasted (went without food):

- King David fasted for seven days when his son was ill (2 Samuel 12:16–18).
- Elijah traveled for forty days and nights without food after an angel fed him (1 Kings 19:8).
- Queen Esther led the Jews in a three-day fast before she approached the king (Esther 4:16).
- Daniel fasted for three weeks before understanding a vision from God (Daniel 10:3).

Exodus 34:29 explains that when Moses came down from the mountain, his face was radiant. That means it gave off light. Moses didn't know that his face was glowing, but the others did. They were afraid and wanted to run from him. Even Moses's brother, Aaron, was afraid to go near him.

Moses called for the people to come and hear what God was telling him. Aaron and the other Israelites came near Moses. They listened to all that God had said.

When Moses finished speaking, he covered his face with a veil. Whenever he went to talk with God, Moses uncovered his face. Whenever he returned to the people, he covered up with the veil again.

As Light as... Iron?

2 Kings 6:1–7

Which of these items floats on water and which ones sink? A feather? A penny? A stone? A soccer ball? An iron axe head? Look at the bottom of the page to find out.

If you've never heard of a floating axe head, you only have to look as far as the Bible. The book of 2 Kings tells of many miracles performed by the prophet Elisha. One of these miracles happened near the Jordan River.

A group of prophets complained to Elisha. "The place where we dwell under your charge is too small for us," they said. "Let us go to the Jordan and each of us get there a log, and let us make a place for us to dwell there" (2 Kings 6:1–2).

Elisha told the prophets to go ahead. One of the prophets convinced Elisha to come along.

When Elisha threw a stick into the water, the heavy iron axe head floated.

Answers: float, sink, sink, float, both

146

At the Jordan River, the prophets got busy chopping down trees. These were most likely not wealthy men. Some did not even own their own tools. One of the men had borrowed an axe for the job.

As the man lifted the axe over his shoulder to swing, the axe head came loose. It soared through the air and landed in the river. He cried out to Elisha, "Alas, my master! It was borrowed" (2 Kings 6:5). How would he be able to pay back the owner for losing the axe head?

Elisha helped the man in an extraordinary way. He didn't wade into the water to find the axe head. He didn't give the man money to buy a new one. Instead, Elisha cut a stick and threw it into the water where the axe head had landed. Suddenly, the heavy iron axe head floated in the water. The man lifted the borrowed axe head out of the water. What a relief!

Ancient Tools

The Bible mentions tools made of stone, iron, bronze, and other materials. Workers used tools to hammer, carve, and punch holes. Soldiers used weapons like swords, spears, and bows and arrows to fight. Farmers used tools to plant, harvest, and process crops.

Bible Index

Art Credits

page 2 givaga/Shutterstock • page 3 David Pereiras/Shutterstock • page 4 AmandaCarden/Shutterstock • page 5 BerrySchlider/Shutterstock • page 6 Armina-Udovenko/DepositPhotos.com • page 7 Alex Mit/Shutterstock • page 8 Linas T/Shutterstock • page 9 Haris McHorror/Shutterstock • page 10 cozmopics. 137/DepositPhotos.com • page 11 tomertu/Shutterstock • page 12 holbox/Shutterstock • page 13 Javier Brosch/Shutterstock • page 14 FRANKHILDEBRAND/Istock • page 15 RichVintage/Istock • page 16 xtock/Istock • page 17 David Tadevosian/Shutterstock • page 18 guteksk7/Shutterstock • page 19 KieferPix/Shutterstock • page 20 vagabond 54/Shutterstock • page 21, 27, 31 ,33, 38, 84 Istockphoto.com • page 22 Subbotina Anna/Shutterstock • page 23 Daniel Prudek/Shutterstock • page 24 fotokris/Istock • page 25 Elnur/Shutterstock • page 26 Dim Dimich/Shutterstock • page 28 zoryanchik/Shutterstock • page 29 marilyna/Istock • page 30 Vladimir Kim/Istock • page 32 Jade ThaiCatwalk/Shutterstock • page 34 valeriebarry/Istock • page 35, 36 James Steidl/Shutterstock • page 37 Anettas/Shutterstock • page 39 Claire Plumridge/Shutterstock • page 40 andipantz/Istock • page 41 vlastas/Shutterstock • page 42 stellalevi/Istock • page 43, 93 TheBiblePeople • page 44 Matt Cornish/Shutterstock • page 45 NatalyaMatveeva/Shutterstock • page 46 Leremy/Shutterstock • page 47 Wavebreak/Istock • page 48 sirastock/Istock • page 49 Jimmy1984/Istock • page 50, 72, 74 Commons.Wikipedia.org • page 51 RealCreation /Istock • page 52 Jolanda Aalbers/Shutterstock • page 53 Stefano Buttafoco/Shutterstock • page 54 Eugene R Thieszen/Shutterstock • page 55 nopow. /Istock • page 56 stuartbur/Istock • page 57 sturti/Istock • page 58 stock_colors/Istock • page 59 ideabug/Istock • page 60 pathdoc/Shutterstock • page 60 PicsFive/DepositPhotos.com • page 61 Valentin Valkov/Shutterstock • page 62 prapann/Shutterstock • page 63 sdominick/Istock • page 64 PongMoji/Shutterstock • page 65 MorganStudio/Shutterstock • page 66 PeteWill/Istock • page 67 cineuno/Shutterstock • page 68 Africa Studio/Shutterstock • page 69 GraphiTect/Shutterstock • page 70 redhumv/Istock • page 71, 85 lolostock/Istock • page 73 Andrea Izzotti/Istock • page 75 Chayanin Wongpracha/Shutterstock • page 76 bowie15/Istock • page 77 3D_generator/Istock • page 78 baona/Istock • page 79 Piyaset/Shutterstock • page 80 monkeybusinessimages/Istock • page 81 GAMARUBA/Shutterstock • page 82 tuulimaa/Istock • page 83 yodiyim/Shutterstock • page 86 Nebojsa Markovic/Shutterstock • page 87 wrangel/Istock • page 88 Rocksweeper/Shutterstock • page 89 Alexandrum79/Istock • page 90 ArtTim/Istock • page 91 sandsun/Istock • page 92 lazyllama/Shutterstock • page 93 Igor Zh./Shutterstock • page 94 KiraVolkov/Istock • page 95 vencavolrab/Istock • page 96 Ig0rZh/Istock • page 97 michaeljung/Shutterstock • page 97 NikitinaOlga 391/DepositPhotos.com • page 98 Bruce Rolff/Shutterstock • page 99 Brzostowska/Shutterstock • page 100 m-gucci/Istock • page 101 Bartosz Hadyniak/Istock • page 102 Ralwel/Istock • page 104 SebastianKnight/Shutterstock • page 105 Alisa24/Shutterstock • page 106 romiri/Istock • page 107 CrossEyedPhotography/Istock • page 108 aldomurillo/Istock • page 109, 115 BibleArtLibrary/Istock • page 110 pengyou91/Istock • page 111 Sabphoto/Shutterstock • page 112 Lacheev/Istock • page 113 AvatarKnowmad/Istock • page 114 RichardUpshur/Istock • page 116 traveler1116/Istock • page 117 heywoody/Istock • page 118 indigolotos/Istock • page 119 RomoloTavani/Istock • page 120 Wolkenengel565/Shutterstock • page 121 Adao/Shutterstock • page 122 Vadim Sadovski/Shutterstock • page 124 Marafona/Shutterstock • page 125 olegganko/Shutterstock • page 126 Dmitry Petrenko/Shutterstock • page 127 Dudarev Mikhail/Shutterstock • page 128 Alexandra Lande/Shutterstock • page 129 Nok Lek/Shutterstock • page 130 Grafissimo/Istock • page 131 flil/Istock • page 132 Instants/Istock • page 133 karimhesham/Istock • page 134 graytown/Istock • page 135 weerapatkiatdumrong/Istock • page 136 Sergio Ponomarev/Shutterstock • page 137 MarianVejcik/Istock • page 138 jsp/Shutterstock • page 139 peeterv/Istock • page 140 stevanovicigor/Istock • page 141 Rost9/Shutterstock • page 142 ChameleonsEye/Shutterstock • page 143 studiovin/Shutterstock • page 144 Kichigin/Shutterstock • page 145 MANDY GODBEHEAR/Shutterstock • page 146 photosmash/Istock • page 147 grafvision/Istock

museum of the Bible

EXPERIENCE THE BOOK THAT SHAPES HISTORY

Museum of the Bible is a 430,000-square-foot building located in the heart of Washington, D.C.—just steps from the National Mall and the U.S. Capitol. Displaying artifacts from several collections, the Museum explores the Bible's history, narrative, and impact through high-tech exhibits, immersive settings, and interactive experiences. Upon entering, you will pass through two massive, bronze gates resembling printing plates from Genesis 1. Beyond the gates, an incredible replica of an ancient artifact containing Psalm 19 hangs behind etched glass panels. Come be inspired by the imagination and innovation used to display thousands of years of biblical history.

Museum of the Bible aims to be the most technologically advanced museum in the world, starting with its unique Digital Guide that allows guests to personalize their museum experience with navigation, customized tours, supplemental visual and audio content, and more.

For more information and to plan your visit, go to
museumofthe**Bible**.org.